THE UNIVERSITY
OF BIRMINGHAM

CONTENTS

Increasing numbers of park and recreation professionals are curious about economic impact studies; are undertaking them within their agencies; or are commissioning them from outside experts. Interest has been stimulated both by recognition of their usefulness in repositioning agencies through demonstrating the contributions of park and recreation services to economic development, and by coincident improvements in software development that have made such studies relatively easy and inexpensive to undertake.

The intent of this publication is to provide information that will enable professionals to better understand how to do good economic impact studies, and to correctly interpret results to their stakeholders. The publication: (1) discusses the role of measuring economic impacts in repositioning the field to enable agencies to acquire more resources; (2) describes the principles of economic impact studies, common abuses of those principles, and the consequences of abuses; (3) discusses how to collect the data needed to calculate economic impact; and (4) reports results from 30 studies undertaken by the author.

Knowledge of economic impacts may be useful for both evaluation and forecasting purposes. The evaluation role is to report the return that a jurisdiction's residents receive on the resources they invest in a given event. The forecasting capability stems from the use of evaluation data gathered in a similar context by previous studies to estimate the likely returns from future events that a jurisdiction may be contemplating bidding for or initiating.

The National Recreation and Park Association is committed to developing a training program that will enable professionals to demonstrate to their stakeholders the contribution made by park and recreation services to a community's economic development. The program consists of documenting the scientific knowledge base; developing training manuals; and training a cadre of instructors who will disseminate the information to their peers. This publication documenting the scientific knowledge base of economic impact studies is the first component of the larger program.

The author is very appreciative of the assistance provided by Seokho Lee who patiently tutored him in the nuances of IMPLAN; undertook the analyses for all the studies reported here; and prepared the illustrations and formatted the narrative for this publication. The studies could not have been undertaken without the financial support and data collection efforts provided by the following:

Mollie Holt, Boise Parks and Recreation Department, Idaho.

Steve Beachy, College Station Parks and Recreation Department, Texas.

Doug Romig, Des Moines Parks and Recreation Department, Iowa.

Curt Marsh, Everett Parks and Recreation Department, Washington.

Linda Lane, Grand Rapids Parks and Recreation Department, Michigan.

Murdock Jemerson, Lansing Parks and Recreation Department, Michigan.

Judy Weiss, Scottsdale Department of Community Services, Arizona.

The support, encouragement and contributions of these park and recreation professionals, their colleagues, and their agencies is very much appreciated.

CHAPTER 1

REPOSITIONING PARK AND RECREATION DEPARTMENTS AS CENTRAL CONTRIBUTORS TO ECONOMIC DEVELOPMENT

In 1991, the notion of benefits-based management was introduced to the field.[1] It represented the managerial application of more than two decades of pioneering work in identifying and measuring outcomes resulting from individuals engaging in recreational activities. Benefits-based management directs that when designing a service or communicating its benefits the focus should be on outcomes rather than on how many came, the cost per head, or who won.

Subsequently, the benefits-based approach was embraced by the National Recreation and Park Association which undertook a vigorous information dissemination effort comprised of training programs, the commissioning of further research, publications, and merchandise bearing the logo, The Benefits are Endless... . The dissemination goals were to communicate the basic principles of the benefits-based approach and to generate awareness of its potential. As a result of this effort, the benefits movement has acquired considerable momentum. One of the lessons learned from implementing it suggests that when the goal is to secure increased allocations of tax dollars, there is virtue in focus-

sing on a relatively small set of collective or "public" benefits, one of which is economic development.

In recent decades, the basis for operating park and recreation programs shifted from the original rationale, which focussed on meritorious social outcomes, to a more narrow notion that such services are provided because particular segments of the population want them.[2] However, the vacuity of this strategy is now apparent to many, and it has become clear that additional resources are likely to be forthcoming only when support for the field extends beyond that of existing participants who directly benefit from the services delivered. User groups have been the dominant focus of agencies' efforts in recent years. Servicing them will always be a central element of the mission, but in many jurisdictions they have proven to be too narrow a constituency for sustaining or securing additional tax resources.

User satisfaction, while necessary, is an inadequate indicator of the success of a park and recreation department when used alone, because it does not incorporate non-users' evaluations of the agency. Most taxpayers are not frequent users of these services. Thus, many of them have difficulty understanding why they should support them. The prevailing sentiment is often: If only some segments of our community use park and recreation services, then why should the rest of us have to pay for them? To gain the support of non-users, an agency has to provide a convincing answer to the fundamental marketing question, "What is in it for them?" Broader community support is likely to be dependent on building awareness not only of the on-site benefits that accrue to users, but also of the off-site benefits that accrue to non-users in communities.

There is increased recognition that while benefit driven programs may lead to higher levels of satisfaction among participants and attract increased numbers, such "private" benefits have relatively little impact on resource allocation decisions made by elected officials. These benefits are described as "private" because they accrue only to program participants and do not extend to the majority of the population who are only occasional users or non-users. Providing resources to a parks and recreation department so a minority of residents can have enjoyable experiences is likely to be a low priority when measured against the critical economic, health, safety and welfare issues with which most legislative bodies are confronted.

To justify the allocation of additional resources, elected officials have to be convinced that park and recreation agencies deliver collective or "public" benefits. These are defined as benefits that accrue to most people in a community, even though they do not participate in an agency's programs or use its facilities. There are just three broad categories of these public benefits: economic development; alleviating social problems; and environmental stewardship.[3] A summary of these categories is given in Appendix 1. However, even these three types of collective

benefits receive funding support only when they are regarded as being high priority in a community. Hence, the task of park and recreation agency managers is to identify which of these public benefits is most prominent on a jurisdiction's political agenda, and to demonstrate the agency's potential contribution to fulfilling that agenda.

This publication focuses on the potential contribution of park and recreation agencies to economic development through their ability to attract visitors. Economic development is a political priority in most communities because it is viewed as a means of enlarging the tax base. The enlargement provides more tax revenues that governments can use either to improve the community's infrastructure, facilities, and services, or to reduce the level of taxes paid by existing residents. It is seen also as a source of jobs and income that enable residents to improve their quality of life.

Although the discussion in this publication is limited to a park and recreation agency's role in attracting visitors, three other ways are described in Appendix 1 in which an agency may contribute to economic development. They are: attracting businesses; attracting retirees; and enhancing real-estate values.

The Concept of Positioning

When an agency thinks in terms of aligning with a politically important issue such as economic development, it is embracing a concept termed positioning. Positioning refers to the place that parks and recreation occupies in the minds of elected officials and the general public relative to their perception of other services that are the field's competitors for public tax dollars. Ries and Trout were the first to articulate the central importance of positioning.[4] They criticized most organizations because they operate as though their services exist in isolation. Some thought there was nothing new in the Ries and Trout contribution because "We have always positioned our services," which demonstrated the legitimacy of the authors' point which was that, "Agencies and organizations don't position services, stakeholders do."

Positioning operates at several levels in a park and recreation agency. In this publication concern is with positioning the agency itself. However, programs and services also can be positioned with respect to competitive alternatives. For example, at the program level the issue may be, "What is the aerobics program's position vis-a-vis those classes offered by other organizations in the area?" The challenge is to identify features that give the program unique or distinctive appeal and differentiate it from those of competitors.

Without competition, positioning would be unnecessary and a good image would probably suffice to attract support and resources. Most park and recreation agencies have a positive image in their communities. Surveys invariably report an overwhelming percentage of residents as being "satisfied" or "very satisfied" with an agency's performance. However, often this does not translate into increased resources, because the agency's performance and importance are evaluated in isolation and are not related to the performance and importance of other agencies with which it is competing for funds. Thinking in terms of position rather than image is more useful because it embraces comparison with competitors. It compares elected officials' and taxpayers' perceptions of the park and recreation agency with those they hold of other public services in which they may invest.

Identifying and establishing a strong, preferred position is the most important strategic decision that park and recreation managers make. It is likely to determine the agency's future. Once it has been made, all subsequent

actions should be geared to implementing it. An established position that reflects responsiveness to a community's central concerns is key to an agency developing and nurturing a broader constituency; securing additional resources; guiding programmatic and facility priorities made by staff and stakeholders; and improving the morale of staff by raising their perceived status in the community. The goal should be to reinforce the desired position by integrating as many of the agency's actions as possible, so each component action fulfills a role in helping to establish the position in the minds of stakeholders.

It has been noted that the provision of park and recreation opportunities for their own sake still lacks political clout.[5] They have to be shown to solve community problems before politicians see them as being worthy of additional funding. The present position of park and recreation services that has existed in the minds of most stakeholders for several decades is that they are relatively discretionary, nonessential services. They are nice to have it they can be afforded after the important, essential services have been funded. It has been observed that:

> Elected officials in the United States and Canada tend to hold the erroneous belief that most to all of the benefits of leisure accrue to the individuals who use leisure services and that there are few to any spin-off benefits from this use to society in general. This contrasts with their views about the social merits of other social services (e.g., education, health services, police and fire protection, transportation) for which these elected officials acknowledge large benefits to society beyond those that accrue to the direct users of those services. Therefore, these officials have improperly adopted for leisure services the principle of public finance, which

dictates that only limited public funds should be allocated to a social service that does not promote the general welfare.[1]

Thus, the key to securing additional resources for park and recreation services is to reposition them so they are perceived as contributing to alleviating problems which constitute the prevailing political concerns of policy makers who are responsible for allocating tax funds. Only when they are so repositioned will park and recreation services be perceived positively as part of the solution to a jurisdiction's problems, rather than being perceived as having no impact or even as being a negative drain on its tax resources.

Positioning implies a commitment to segmentation. In this publication, the selected focus is on economic development which means that market segments, services and facilities that did not contribute to strengthening this position would not be emphasized or prioritized. The agency is likely to be successful in establishing a distinct position to the extent that it is not constrained by the need to dissipate energies elsewhere. The selection of which issue an agency elects to focus upon, depends on the community's priorities and the agency's personnel and facility resources. The preferred position should be the optimum "selling idea" for motivating taxpayers and elected officials to allocate additional resources for parks and recreation.

A cardinal rule is that an agency should position itself by aligning with only one or at the very most two community issues, since establishing a position in residents' minds requires prolonged focus. This is because in order to manage the cacophony of information to which they are now exposed, individuals limit their intake to the minimum they need to get by. Hence, they tend to know a small amount about many things, but they don't know much about anything. This applies to the mission of a park and recreation agency equally as well as it does to any other public agency, private organization, or commercial business.

To residents, perceptions are truth. Their perceptions may not be correct, especially those of non-users who have little contact with a park and recreation agency, but it is what they know and they have no reason to make an effort to know more. Thus, most taxpayers are unlikely to pay much attention to the details, subtleties and complexities of a park and recreation agency's mission. In the age of the "soundbite," focus is everything. The message has to be pervasive. The best an agency can hope for is that an occasional piece of information may penetrate to reinforce or amend residents' existing perceptions. Hence, the value of consistency over time in program emphasis and in communication messages cannot be overemphasized. Without concentrating resources to support the selected repositioning strategy, it will not succeed. Aligning with multiple issues may be tempting, but such efforts are unlikely to be successful. The probable outcome of diffusing resources by aligning with multiple issues is that no clear identity will be established, and that a fuzzy, confused position similar to that which currently exists will emerge.

Positioning reflects people's beliefs and value systems which are hard to change because they define who individuals are. Thus, repositioning is a difficult task because it involves shifting a widely held, long-established attitude towards the field. Further, there are pragmatic difficulties in shifting to this mode. An agency cannot immediately abandon many of its current tasks and switch those resources to strengthen its repositioning efforts. If this was done, there would probably be a loud outcry from existing clienteles. Such shifts can only be implemented over time. Agencies should think in terms of a 10 year, rather than a 1 year, time horizon to accomplish repositioning. After all, that is probably the minimum time period for which stakeholders have held the existing position of park and recreation services being relatively discretionary and non-essential. Although repositioning is likely to take many years of effort, the imperative to initiate it was articulated by the commentator who observed: "The divide in government between 'essential' and 'non-essential' service is going to get greater and greater. We are standing in the middle of that divide and need to jump as it widens".[6]

The Set of Repositioning Strategies

There are three strategies that agencies can pursue to achieve this repositioning.[7] They are not mutually exclusive; rather, all three should be embraced simultaneously. The first strategy is *real repositioning*, which means that an agency changes what it does so that desired community priority needs are met through its offerings. This may be achieved by adopting a more aggressive entrepreneurial approach to soliciting tourism business for the community.

This could involve developing packaged services for visitors. For example, in every area there are numerous organizations that have a program chair whose challenge is to develop a program of activities for the group. Park and recreation agencies have a smorgasbord of offerings available to meet those groups' programming needs. Managing facilities and services does not stop at the front gate! The challenge is not merely to provide services that people want; it is to package them so they can be accessed conveniently. Packaging means that the agency links with a transportation source and necessary support services, such as a restaurant and hotel (if an overnight stay is involved), and offers a fixed price for the total experience to targeted groups. Thus, if an agency offers a fishing trip to senior citizen groups, the package may include a chartered bus, lunch, fishing poles, and a staff person who meets the chartered bus and provides interpretation and assistance with bait, fishing, cleaning fish, and so forth. Targeting groups from outside of the community with packages would help to reposition an agency as a central contributor to tourism and economic development.

Real repositioning may involve not only changing its program offerings but also changing the types of alliances and partnerships that the agency forms, and changing the community forums in which it becomes involved. Allying with other agencies or organizations that already have a firm, well-crystallized image and position may provide a park and recreation agency with a bridging reference point to the position it is seeking. If someone wants to know where a particular address is located, it is much easier to say "next to the tourism agency" if that location is well-known, than to describe the various streets to take to get there!

Thus, strengthening linkages with a jurisdiction's tourism agency may also be an effective real repositioning strategy. If that organization has a positive position in stakeholders' minds, then closer links with it by a park and recreation agency are likely to lead to some of its positive position being conveyed to the agency by association. Real positioning could involve actively partnering with the community tourism agency to create new events designed to attract outside visitors to stay in the jurisdiction for multiple days. Such linkages make pragmatic sense because the two organizations often have complementary assets. Tourism agencies typically have funds available for promotion and such funds are scarce at most park and recreation agencies. In contrast, tourism agencies rarely become involved in directly producing programs and services. Thus, some departments, for example, cooperate with tourism agencies to fund special-event coordinators who are responsible for organizing and soliciting sponsorship for special events in the community. The tourism agencies recognize that park and recreation departments have the expertise and a mandate to organize special events, but frequently lack the funds to launch and promote them effectively. Hence, tourism agencies help fund such positions, provide initial seed funds for some events, and promote all events.

Real positioning is the foundation upon which all actions rest. An agency must not try to be something it is not. It is important that it is able to deliver the outcomes which it promises. If it aligns with economic development, an agency must structure its services and engage in cooperative partnerships that are compatible with its alignment promises.

The second strategy is *competitive repositioning*. This means altering stakeholders' beliefs about what an agency's competitors do. For example, in many communities a convention and visitors bureau is charged with the primary responsibility for attracting visitors. The bureaus frequently imply that the economic impact from all visitors is attributable to their efforts. In this way, they have positioned themselves in the minds of stakeholders as important contributors to economic development, and they receive resources commensurate with that favorable position. As we shall see in chapter 2, this substantially overstates their contribution because many visitors would come even if there was no convention and visitors bureau, while others are there because of the park and recreation agency's efforts rather than those of the bureau. If the discrepancies between the established psychological position of bureaus and reality are subtly pointed out, then re-

sources that would otherwise be appropriated to the convention and visitors bureau may instead be allocated to the parks and recreation agency to develop additional events or facilities that will attract visitors.

Psychological repositioning is the third strategy. This type of repositioning means altering stakeholders' beliefs about what an agency currently does. In many agencies, existing services and facilities already attract an extensive number of visitors to the community. In these cases, the primary strategy should be psychological repositioning which involves documenting, demonstrating and informing stakeholders of the economic benefits that accrue. Since associating parks and recreation services with economic development is a very different perspective from that which prevails in most communities, the results of such studies may be viewed as interesting and newsworthy which would facilitate communication of them by the media to stakeholders.

It has been suggested that park and recreation agencies have a labeling problem.[8] Agencies are labeled based on the means used, i.e., recreation, rather than the ends that they aspire to achieve, e.g., contributing to economic development. In the past two decades, emphasis was placed on providing the means, while the ends were forgotten. Psychological repositioning involves bringing outcomes to the forefront so that when the words parks and recreation are mentioned, people immediately think of them as wanted outcomes or benefits. This is illustrated effectively in the area of tourism where public investments in promoting tourism or developing new tourism opportunities are associated in people's minds with economic development, which most consider to be a highly desirable outcome. Consider the following example:

The city had plenty of money for economic development, but the council could not be persuaded to commit $1.5 million for a 150 acre youth athletic field complex for which there was a clearly demonstrated need. The proposed site was adjacent to two major highways and would be well suited for tournaments in such sports as soccer, rugby, baseball, softball, tennis, and lacrosse. Hence, after an initial rejection by the council, the project's supporters regrouped and repositioned the project as an outdoor special-events center. This terminology resonated with the council and taxpayers because the city had both an existing indoor special-events center and a conference center, and they were recognized widely to be good investments in economic development because of the nonresident visitors which they attracted. Representatives of the hotel-motel association, restaurant association, convention and visitors bureau, and chamber of commerce came to a council meeting to lobby for the athletic complex because its supporters pointed out that the city could hold frequent tournaments bringing 300 to 500 people to the community each weekend from out-of-town. Once it was repositioned into this economic development context and viewed as an outdoor special-events center, the council approved resources to acquire the site. They also recommended that some hotel-motel tax funds be used for this purpose, reducing the amount needed from taxpayers.

Another strategy for psychological repositioning is to take advantage of the positive position that tourism organizations in many communities have established in stakeholders' minds by making extensive use of the vocabulary of "tourism". The extreme case would be a change in the department's name that better reflected an agency's central contribution to tourism in the community. A name such as the department of parks, recreation, and tourism, or the department of recreation amenities and attractions may achieve that end. If political considerations make such a change non-feasible, then constant reference to the "recreation and tourism industry" and to the "tourism" services provided by the agency may enable a park and recreation agency to build a bridge to tourism's established position. Over time, this is likely to lead to some of the positive connotations and aura associated with tourism being transferred to the park and recreation agency.

Parks and Recreation Agencies as the Engines of Tourism

Tourism is not recognized as an official industry in the Census Bureau's Standard Industrial Classification system. The Classification recognizes hotel, restaurant, airline, automobile, shipping, retail and advertising industries, along with many others that are involved in meeting the needs and desires of various types of travelers, but it does not include tourism as an industry. The inappropriateness of using the term "tourism industry" has been explained in the following terms:

> Although it is common to hear or read references to the "tourism industry," such a phrase is problematic because tourism is not an industry in the conventional sense. It is not an industry because its components (individual businesses) do not provide a common product or service and they do not use the same fundamental technology.[9]

The tourism "industry" is a generic umbrella

term that advocates derive by aggregating the outputs from an arbitrary combination of dozens of recognized industries. From an economist's perspective, treating tourism as a distinctive industry causes double-counting, because the outputs of those businesses that advocates subsume under the tourism industry are already officially allocated to different industries. Such "industry" data are contrived and meaningless.

The broad field of travel is commonly divided into four major segments based upon purpose of trip. They are (i) business-related travel; (ii) personal business, including visiting friends or relatives; (iii) conventions and meetings; and (iv) pleasure travel. There is some overlap between these trip purpose segments. For example, while the primary trip purpose may be attending a convention or visiting friends and relatives, this may be integrated with pleasure activities. Traditionally, the term "tourist" referred only to pleasure travelers and did not embrace the other three trip purposes. The inclination of most public tourism agencies and private tourism advocacy groups today is to extend the definition of tourism to include all these segments, since the broader it is defined, the more visitors it embraces and the larger its economic value is perceived to be. This leads to enhancement of the stature and visibility of those in a community associated with tourism, enabling them to position themselves more favorably in the psyche of both the general public and legislators.

Tourism agencies are unlikely to have any influence on business travel or on visiting friends and relatives/personal business. The

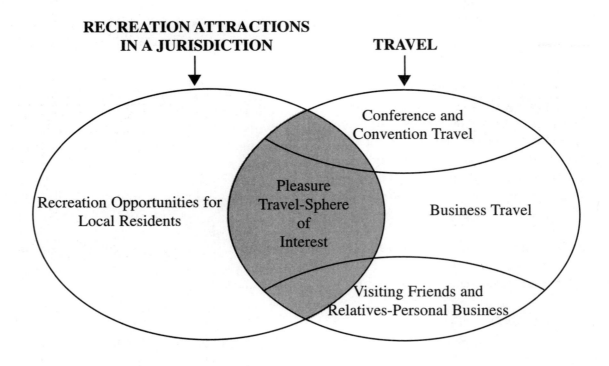

Figure 1. Segments of Travel and Their Inter-relationship

two segments of travel that are most likely to be responsive to their efforts are conference and convention travel, and pleasure travel. The shaded area in Figure 1 indicates that this latter segment is a primary sphere of interest and influence for park and recreation agencies. It is in this area, where recreation attractions are the primary purpose of travel, that park and recreation agencies often can claim to be the primary engine that drives tourism economic impact in a community.

Figure 2 shows a simplified model of a tourism system. It indicates that visitors use some mode of transportation (e.g., automo-bile or airplane) to leave their homes and travel to attractions, which are supported by various kinds of services (e.g., hotels/motels, restaurants, retailing). The attractions and support services provide information and promote their offerings to target groups whom they have identified as potential visitors.

This tourism system is activated by attractions. Only in rare cases do people leave their home milieu and travel some distance by automobile, airplane, or ship because they want to stay in a particular hotel or dine at a particular restaurant in a different locale.

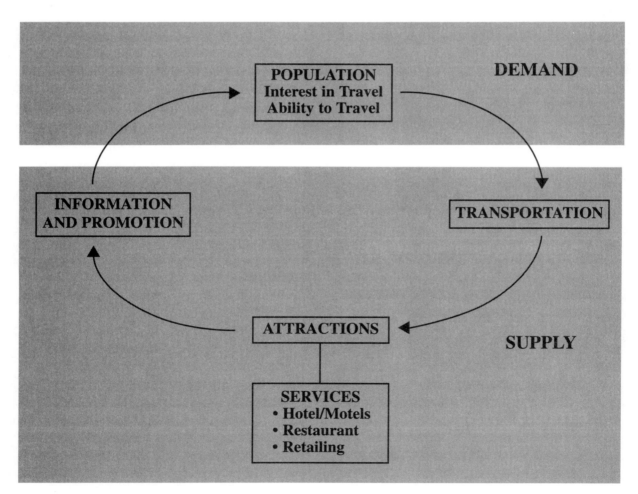

Figure 2. A Simplified Model of a Tourism System

Table 1	A Taxonomy of Tourist Attractions
Arts	Theaters, Art Galleries, Museums, Performing groups, Music concerts
Heritage Places	Ethnic cultural places, Shrines/churches, Historical sites and structures, Educational instructions, Industry factory tours
Parks	National, State, Regional, Local, Beaches, Theme parks
Recreation	Events and festivals, Aquatic and coastals areas, Outdoor recreations (e.g., camping, fishing, hunting), Sports, (e.g., golf, tennis, skiing, sailing, softball), Fitness and wellness centers
Arenas	College sports, Professional franchises, Concerts and exhibitions
Other	Gambling places, Cruise ships

Most of the time, the desire to go to a destination on a pleasure trip is stimulated by its attractions.

A taxonomy of attractions likely to activate pleasure travel is shown in Table 1. A perusal of this list of tourist attractions leads to the conclusion that almost all of them are developed, and in most cases are operated, by the public sector or by nonprofit organizations. A large proportion of them are likely to be the responsibility of park and recreation agencies. This leads to the conclusion that *in most communities, pleasure travel is a business that the public sector drives, and park and recreation agencies are central to that business*. Thus, in most communities, park and recreation agencies are the engines of tourism.

This central role in tourism is not part of the position that park and recreation agencies occupy in stakeholders' minds. Indeed, it is the antithesis of the general public's and tourism field's conventional wisdom. Most people are under the misapprehension that tourism is the almost exclusive preserve of the commercial sector. The commercial sec-tor offers essential transportation; support services, such as accommodations, restaurants, and retailing; and information and promotion dissemination (see Figure 2). However, in most communities the public sector is the primary provider of the attractions that activate pleasure travel.

The popular perception of tourist attractions is dominated by glamorous, large-scale, commercial developments such as Disney-World, Disneyland, other theme parks, cruise ships, casinos, Las Vegas, and all-inclusive resort hotels. However, in terms of annual visitor days, such attractions account for only a small percentage of pleasure travel in the United States. DisneyWorld and Disneyland may attract more than 40 million visitors per year, but this number represents only 12% of the visitor days recorded in the national parks and less than 3% of visitor days at all federal recreational areas (including those operated by the U.S. Forest Service, U.S. Army Corps of Engineers, National Park Service, U.S. Fish and Wildlife Service, and Bureau of Land Management). The annual number of visits to state parks is approximately 740 million, and this number, in turn, is minuscule when compared with the number of visitors to regional, county, and local parks and beaches.

Very few communities have large scale commercial tourist attractions. Despite their absence, most jurisdictions recognize the importance of tourism to economic development and establish convention and visitor bureaus or similar agencies, whose primary mission is to attract visitors. They invariably rely on the park and recreation agency to create attractions that will persuade visitors to come to the community and spend money there. The extent to which the park and recreation agency constitutes the engine of tourism in any particular community can be ascertained by listing all the programs, festi-

vals, tournaments, competitions and facilities operated or co-sponsored by the parks and recreation department that attract pleasure travelers to the community from out-of-town. Similar lists should be developed for non-profit organizations and for commercial attractions. In most communities, the commercial attractions list will be the shortest. In such cases, this **competitive repositioning** strategy will show the relative insignificance of commercial enterprises in attracting visitors to the community when compared to the public sector attractions. The dissemination of such comparative lists may make an effective contribution to repositioning parks and recreation as being central to tourism in the minds of stakeholders.

CHAPTER 2

UNDERSTANDING THE PRINCIPLES OF ECONOMIC IMPACT STUDIES

At the end of a financial year, a tourism agency typically reports to the city council that the (say) $500,000 which was invested in its operation (usually from a bed tax) was responsible for an economic impact of (say) $30 million which the jurisdiction received from tourism. The agency director is likely to conclude her presentation to the council by stating, "For every $1 you invested in us, the community received $60 in return." Such claims are rarely challenged and the apparent high return on the investment is widely accepted by legislators, the media, and the general public. However, it was noted in the previous chapter that the local tourism agency's contribution is likely to be substantial only in the convention and conference segment of travel. A large proportion of the claimed tourism economic impact is attributable to business travel or to visiting friends and relatives. A tourism agency is unlikely to make any meaningful contribution to increasing visitors in these two segments.

Similarly, tourism agencies' claims to ownership of the economic impact attributable to pleasure travel are unwarranted. In some instances, these agencies contribute funds for promotion, but a plethora of tour-

ism studies report that the dominant source of information to tourists is word-of-mouth. Hence, most pleasure travel visitation should be attributable to those responsible for providing and operating public recreation attractions, and relatively little to those whose responsibility is limited to a supportive role in publicizing it. Since public park and recreation agencies provide a majority of the recreation attractions in many communities, most economic impact accruing from pleasure travel is directly attributable to their operations.

The challenge, then, is to identify the economic impact that is attributable to attractions provided by a park and recreation agency and to claim ownership of it. When the parks and recreation department in city A reported the financial consequences of hosting a national softball championship tournament, it reported a loss of $9,375. When the convention and visitors bureau in that community reported the consequences of hosting the same event, it reported an economic gain to the community of $525,000. It is obvious which agency was likely to be viewed most positively by elected officials and taxpayers.

Why did two agencies report such disparate data from the same event? The answer to this question is that they used different approaches for demonstrating accountability for their public funds.

Park and recreation agencies traditionally have provided *financial* reports, while the tradition in the tourism field has been to provide *economic* reports. The different reporting methods have resulted in the two types of agencies occupying very different positions in the minds of public officials. By using economic reports, many convention and visitor bureaus have persuaded elected officials and decision-makers that they are central contributors to their communities' economic health. In contrast, park and recreation agencies generally have not been successful in creating a similar central position in decision-makers' minds regarding the economic contribution of their services, because they have used only financial reports. Hence, in a climate of fiscal conservatism, park and recreation agencies are mistakenly perceived to be "black hats" whose services result in net economic losses to the community, while convention and visitor bureaus have established themselves as "white hats" because they bring new money into the community.

These perspectives are fallacious. To change them and to reposition themselves more favorably, park and recreation agencies must emulate the methods used by tourism agencies and identify the *economic* impact that is attributable to the facilities and services they provide.

The Rationale for Economic Impact Studies

Figure 3 illustrates the conceptual reasoning for developing economic balance sheets to supplement financial information. It shows that residents of a community "give"

funds to their city council in the form of taxes. The city council uses a proportion of these funds to subsidize production of an event or development of a facility. The facility or event attracts nonresident visitors who spend money in the local community both inside and outside of the events and facilities that they visit. This new money from outside of the community creates income and jobs in the community for residents. This completes the virtuous cycle of economic development. Community residents are responsible for providing the initial funds, and they receive a return on their investment in the form of new jobs and more household income.

A park and recreation agency essentially provides seed money and in-kind resources to leverage substantial economic gains for the community. If public sector resources are not used to financially underwrite the cost of staging these events, then the consequent economic benefits to the local community will not accrue. Private enterprises are unlikely to commit funds to organizing such events, because they are unable to capture a large enough proportion of the income spent by participants to obtain a satisfactory return on their investment.

The traditional financial balance sheet presented by park and recreation agencies assumes that the cycle shown in Figure 3 starts and ends with the city council, rather than with a community's residents. This is narrow and misleading because it includes only the taxes and revenues that accrue to local government from the event or facility. Such a narrow definition suggests that concern should be focussed on income accruing to the council from lease fees, admission revenues, increased sales tax revenues, and other revenue sources. However, this approach is flawed conceptually because the money invested does not belong to the council; rather, it belongs to the city's residents. Although it is efficient for the residents' investment to be

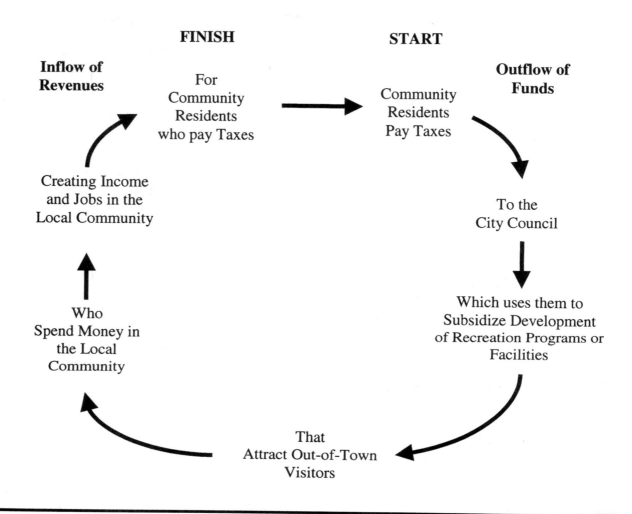

FINISH   **START**

Inflow of   For   Community   **Outflow of**
Revenues   Community   Residents   **Funds**
                      Residents   Pay Taxes
                     who pay Taxes

Creating Income   To the
and Jobs in the   City Council
Local Community

Who   Which uses them to
Spend Money in   Subsidize Development
the Local   of Recreation Programs or
Community   Facilities

                          That
                  Attract Out-of-Town
                       Visitors

Figure 3. The Conceptual Rationale for Developing an Economic Balance Sheet

funneled through the council, the return that *residents* receive is what is important, not merely the proportion of the total return that filters back to the council. The purpose of economic impact studies is to measure the economic return to residents.

The difference between the financial and economic approaches is illustrated in Table 2. The park and recreation department's financial balance sheet shows a net loss of $9,375 from the tournament. However, if the agency used an economic balance sheet, as tourism agencies do, then it would show a

net return of $273,000, $511,000, or $150,000 depending on whether economic impact was reported in terms of direct expenditures, sales impact, or impact on personal incomes. (These figures were calculated by taking the gross amounts shown and subtracting from them the $14,000 net cost to taxpayers of hosting the event.)

The capital cost of the softball complex was approximately $2 million, which means that, if the personal income measure of economic impact was used (the reasons for preferring this measure are discussed later in the

Table 2   A Comparison of the Economic Return and the Financial Return to City A from an Amateur Softball Associations Men's 40 and Over Fast-Pitch National Tournament

Context

All 37 teams that qualified for the tournament were from outside the local area. The average number of players per team was 15. Some players brought family and friends with them, so the average size of the contingent associated with each team, including the players, was 21. Because it was an elimination tournament, the length of time that the teams stayed in the community varied from two to six nights.

Economic Return

A survey of the players revealed the following:

Total expenditures in the local area by players and their family and friends	$287,000

An input-output model that calculated multipliers concluded the following:

Total economic impact on sales	$525,000
Total economic impact on personal income	$164,000

Financial Return

Income to the city parks and recreation department from entry fees	$ 4,625
Costs incurred by the department, including manpower, to host the event	$ 14,000
Net financial loss to the city	$ 9,375

Pay-Back Period

The cost of constructing the softball complex was almost $2 million. Based on economic return to residents in terms of personal income, the capital cost of the complex would be repaid after 14 similar tournaments.

chapter), the investment would pay for itself after 14 similar tournaments. How many other investments is a jurisdiction likely to have that pay for themselves in two years (assuming seven tournaments per year) and that continue to contribute $1 million to residents annually for the next 20 years? Agencies that present these kind of data in the form of an economic balance sheet to their stakeholders, demonstrating their contribution to economic development, are likely to reposition themselves favorably in the minds of legislators and the general public.

The Basic Principles of Economic Impact Studies

Because economic impact studies use complex procedures and produce quantifiable outcomes, often there is a presumption in the minds of "bottom-line" oriented audiences who are unfamiliar with the technique, that the analyses are "scientific" and, hence, the outputs are objective and unequivocal. This is fallacious. They offer a misleading guise of statistical sophistication. Economic impact analysis is an inexact process and output numbers should be regarded as a "best guess" rather than as being inviolably accurate. Indeed, if a study was undertaken by five different individuals, then it is probable that there would be five different results.

There are several points in an analysis where underlying assumptions can be made which will substantially impact the final result. Unfortunately, this means there is a temptation to adopt inappropriate procedures and assumptions in order to generate high economic impact numbers that will position an agency more favorably in the minds of elected officials. Sometimes such errors are the result of a genuine lack of understanding of economic impact analysis and the procedures used in it, but in other instances they are committed deliberately and mischievously to generate large numbers and mislead stakeholders.

Most research projects are predicated on a search for truth, but the goal in economic impact studies is less auspicious; it is to legitimize a position. Usually, they are undertaken in order to justify a public expenditure in quantitative dollar terms, with the expectation that the results will reinforce the case for sustaining or increasing resources allocated to the service. In these circumstances, there is a temptation to manipulate the procedures to strengthen the case. Ostensibly, the people hired to conduct economic impact studies appear to be both expert and neutral. However, one commentator has characterized these individuals in the following terms:

They are in truth the exact equivalent of an expert witness in a lawsuit who comes to testify in support of the side that is paying the expert's bill. An expert whose testimony harms his employer's case doesn't get much repeat business. The commentator goes on to state, "The fees for the study are like a religious tithe paid to a priest to come

bless some endeavor".[10]

This type of cynical comment about the integrity of economic studies is becoming increasingly pervasive, because of the extravagant claims for the impact of visitor spending that many of these studies have made. The intent in this section of this publication is to arm park and recreation managers with sufficient knowledge of basic principles that they will be able to identify studies which are ethically challenged and distance themselves from them.

In addition to undertaking economic impact studies for numerous tourism and park and recreation agencies, the author has been involved in reviewing studies commissioned by cities seeking to attract or retain professional sport franchises. The mischievous use of these studies was exemplified a few years ago by the contrasting values placed on the San Francisco Giants baseball franchise when it seemed probable that the team would leave Candlestick Park for a new stadium in San Jose. San Francisco and San Jose are similarly sized cities located only 50 miles apart. In San Francisco, which anticipated losing the franchise if voters in San Jose agreed to fund the stadium, the city's budget director reported that she could document only a $3.1 million net gain to the city from the Giants. She placed this in the context of the city's gross economic product of $30 billion, and pointed out this was 10,000 times as large, to emphasize how insignificant were the economic benefits. A professor of economics at nearby Stanford University was quoted as saying, "Opening a branch of Macy's has a greater economic impact". In contrast, the mayor of San Jose, who was trying to persuade that city's residents to approve a referendum which would authorize $265 million of public funds to build a new stadium in which the Giants would play, announced the results of a study showing that the same franchise would deliver to San Jose somewhere between $50 million and $150 million a year in economic benefits!

In this section five principles central to the integrity of economic impact analyses are reviewed. They are: (a) exclusion of local residents; (b) exclusion of "time-switchers" and "casuals"; (c) use of income rather than sales output measures of economic impact; (d) use of multiplier coefficients rather than multipliers; and (e) careful interpretation of employment measures. Mischievous manipulation of analyses invariably involves abusing one or more of these five principles.

(a) Exclusion of Local Residents

Economic impact attributable to a sports tournament, or special event relates only to new money injected into an economy by visitors, media, vendors, external government entities, or banks and investors from outside the community. Only those visitors who reside outside the jurisdiction and whose primary motivation for visiting is to attend the event, or who stay longer and spend more because of the event, should be included in an economic impact study.

Expenditures by those who reside in the community do not contribute to an event's economic impact because these expenditures represent a recycling of money that already existed there. It is probable that if local residents had not spent this money at the tournament or event, then they would have disposed of it either now or later by purchasing other goods and services in the community. Twenty dollars spent by a local family at a community event is likely to be twenty less dollars spent on movie tickets or other entertainment elsewhere in the community. Thus, expenditures associated with the event by local residents are likely merely to be switched spending, which offers no net eco-

nomic stimulus to the community. Hence, it should not be included when estimating economic impact.

This widespread admonition from economists to disregard locals' expenditures is frequently ignored because when expenditures by local residents are omitted, the economic impact numbers become too small to be politically useful. To rectify this, two disconcerting new terms have emerged. Some agencies now report that their event contributed $X million "to local economic activity." Along with "economic activity" the synonymous term "economic surge" is now being used. Both of these terms are used to describe *all* expenditures associated with an event or facility, irrespective of whether they derive from residents or from out-of-town visitors. This generates the high numbers that study sponsors invariably seek, but the economic surge or economic activity figures are meaningless. They are used by advocates to deliberately mislead stakeholders for the purpose of boosting their advocacy position, because most elected officials, media representatives, and residents mistakenly assume that "economic activity" and "economic surge" are synonymous with measures of economic impact.

If there is evidence to suggest that an event keeps some residents at home who would otherwise leave the area for a trip, then these local expenditures could legitimately be considered as an economic impact since money has been retained in the host community that would otherwise have been spent outside it. However, such evidence is very difficult to collect and is likely to be tenuous, so the accepted convention by economists is to disregard all expenditures by local residents and to recognize that the resultant impact figure may be somewhat conservative.

ing money in the first round of spending, and in successive rounds that did not leak out of the community, will continue to spend this money in the same six ways. The visitors' initial expenditure is likely to go through numerous rounds as it seeps through the economy, with portions of it leaking out each round until it declines to a negligible amount. These subsequent rounds of economic activity reflecting spending by local interindustry purchases and local government revenues (Figure 4) are termed *indirect* impacts.

The proportion of household income that is spent locally on goods and services is termed an *induced* impact, which is defined as the increase in economic activity generated by local consumption due to increases in employee compensation, proprietary income and other property income. The *indirect* and *induced* effects together are frequently called secondary impacts. In summary, there are three elements that contribute to the total impact of a given initial injection of expendi-

tures from out-of-town visitors.

Direct Effects: The first round effect of visitor spending, that is, how much the restauranteurs, hoteliers, and others who received the initial dollars spend on goods and services with other industries in the local economy and pay employees, self-employed individuals and shareholders who live in the jurisdiction.

Indirect Effects: The ripple effect of additional rounds of recirculating the initial visitors' dollars by local businesses and local government.

Induced Effects: Further ripple effects generated by the direct and indirect effects, caused by employees of impacted businesses spending some of their salaries and wages in other businesses in the city.

These three different effects are illustrated in Table 3. In city A in Table 3, each dollar spent by visitors on food and beverages gen-

Table 3   Multiplier Coefficient for Sales (Output) and Personal Income in Two Cities with Different Sized Populations

	Sales (Output) Coefficients						Personal Income Coefficients					
	City A			City B			City A			City B		
	D	D+ID	D+ID +IDU	D	D+ID	D+ID +IDU	D	D+ID	D+ID +IDU	D	D+ID	D+ID +IDU
Food & Beverages	1	1.24	1.91	1	1.32	2.53	.31	.37	.55	.32	.39	.76
Retail Shopping	1	1.20	2.17	1	1.19	3.06	.32	.37	.64	.31	.36	.93
Lodging	1	1.33	1.87	1	1.36	2.44	.28	.36	.51	.32	.42	.75
Private Auto	1	1.22	1.56	1	1.25	1.89	.30	.35	.44	.32	.38	.58
Car Rental	1	1.32	1.65	1	1.34	2.12	.21	.29	.39	.18	.28	.52

D: Direct Effect   **ID:** Indirect Effect   **IDU:** Induced Effect

erated 24 cents in indirect sales and another 67 cents in induced sales. The induced effects stem from household spending of income earned from the direct and indirect effects. Similarly in city A, each dollar spent on food and beverages generated 31 cents in the local community in direct personal income, another 6 cents in indirect personal income, and 18 cents in induced income.

Frequently, studies apply a multiplier coefficient to direct spending estimates without explanation as to how it was derived or how appropriate it is to that particular community, so the naive stakeholder is left with the feeling that there is some magical process through which one dollar of spending eventually turns into two and perhaps even three. The great danger in the multiplier concept, and the way it is presented in research reports aimed at the policy maker, is that its basic concept and application are deceptively simple. However, the data and analyses needed to accurately measure a multiplier are complex and the results require careful interpretation and explanation.

Interpreting Alternative Measures of Economic Impact

Four different types of economic impact measures are commonly reported, and all of them use multiplier coefficients. They are sales, personal income, value added and employment. Because the first three of these are all measured in dollars, they are often confused. A *sales or output* measure reports the direct, indirect, and induced effect of an extra unit of visitor spending on economic activity within a host community. It relates visitor expenditure to the increase in business turnover that it creates. It is a rather esoteric measure with very limited practical value. It may be of some interest to economists interested in researching industry interdependencies; to business proprietors interested in sales impacts; or to officials in governmental

entities who are interested in approximating sales revenues which may accrue from injections of funds into particular sectors, but it does not offer insights that are useful for guiding policy decisions of local elected officials.

The *personal income* measure of economic impact reports the direct, indirect, and induced effect of an extra unit of visitor spending on the changes that result in level of personal income in the host community. In contrast to the sales output indicator, the income measure has substantial practical implications for stakeholders because it enables them to relate the economic benefits received by residents to the costs they invested (Figure 3). The income coefficient reports the income per dollar of direct sales that accrues to residents and it includes employee compensation and proprietor income. The *value added* measure is more expansive than the personal income indicator in that it includes other property income and indirect business taxes, in addition to employee compensation and proprietary income.

Table 3 reports the sales output and personal income indicators derived from two of the economic impact studies reported later in this publication. The table illustrates two points that are crucial to properly interpreting and communicating economic impact measures. First, the coefficients are different for each category of expenditure that is listed. Thus, in city A, a $1 expenditure by visitors on gasoline (private auto) yielded substantially less personal income to residents than a similar $1 expenditure on retail shopping (44 cents compared to 64 cents). However, it should not be assumed that the industry sectors with the highest multiplier coefficients contribute most to the local economy, because high volume of expenditures in a sector may compensate for a relatively low multiplier. Sectors with high multiplier values in which there are low levels of spending, may not be as valuable as sectors with low multiplier values that have high levels of spending.

The second key point illustrated in Table 3 is that the values of *sales* indicators are substantially higher than those of *personal income* measures. For example, the table indicates that on average in city A, each $1 expenditure by visitors on accommodations will generate 51 cents in personal income for residents of the city, but business activity in the city is likely to rise by $1.87. If analysts do not clearly define which economic impact measure is being discussed, then there is a danger that inaccurate, exaggerated, spurious inferences will be drawn from the data.

In an analysis of a park and recreation agency special event, sports tournament or facility, sales measures of economic impact are unlikely to be of interest to local residents. The point of interest is likely to be the impact of visitors' expenditures on residents' personal incomes. Most government officials and taxpayers are likely to be interested only in knowing how much extra income residents will receive from the injection of funds from visitors. Their interest in value of sales *per se* is likely to be limited, since it does not directly impact residents' standard of living. Further, the use of sales indicators may give a false impression of the true impacts of visitor spending, because the highest effects on personal income are not necessarily generated from the highest increases in sales.

The conceptual model shown in Figure 3, which illustrates the rationale for economic impact studies, specifies that their purpose is to compare how much money residents invest in a park and recreation event or facility, with how much income they receive from it. The notion of sales transactions does not appear anywhere in the model and, from the perspective of residents and elected officials, it is irrelevant to the analysis. Nevertheless, because sales measures of economic impact are frequently three or more times larger than personal income indicators (Table 3), sponsors of economic impact studies invariably report economic impact in terms of sales outputs rather than personal income. The higher numbers appear to better justify the public investment that is being advocated, but they are meaningless for this purpose.

(d) Use of Multiplier Coefficients Rather than Multipliers

The term "multiplier" is commonly applied to two different types of measures derived from the multiplier process and this has created substantial confusion among practitioners, commentators and researchers. Only one of these indices for which the term multiplier is used is of value to policy makers and it is actually a *multiplier coefficient* rather than a multiplier. It is calculated by the following formula:

$$\frac{\text{Direct} + \text{Indirect} + \text{Induced Effects}}{\text{Injected Visitor Expenditures}}$$

Table 4A reports summary multiplier coefficients for the six industrial sectors in which out-of-town visitors spent their money in the seven communities in which the economic impact studies reported in this publication were undertaken. Interpolating the numbers from city A in Table 4A to the formula indicates that the total personal income coefficient is .65:

$$\frac{.36 + .08 + .21}{1} = .65$$

This personal income coefficient indicates that for every $1 injected by visitors into the economy of city A, 65 cents of personal income accrues in the form of employee wages and salaries, and proprietary income.

Table 4A Summary **Multiplier Coefficients** for the Six Industries on Which There Were Visitor Expenditures in the Seven Study Cities

City	Sales			Personal Income			Jobs		
	Direct	Direct + Indirect	Direct + Indirect + Induced	Direct	Direct + Indirect	Direct + Indirect + Induced	Direct	Direct + Indirect	Direct + Indirect + Induced
A	1.00	1.26	1.88	.36	.44	.65	27.71	31.36	42.07
B	1.00	1.28	2.29	.42	.51	.90	28.87	32.57	48.46
C	1.00	1.26	1.78	.37	.46	.65	25.53	28.91	36.64
D	1.00	1.29	2.41	.39	.48	.89	26.78	30.94	49.38
E	1.00	1.22	1.83	.38	.45	.66	22.11	24.96	33.81
F	1.00	1.29	2.12	.38	.48	.80	24.39	28.18	40.68
G	1.00	1.22	2.15	.40	.47	.82	22.78	25.59	38.93

D: Direct Effect   **ID**: Indirect Effect   **IDU**: Induced Effect

In contrast, the formula for deriving a *multiplier* has a different denominator. It is:

$$\frac{\text{Direct + Indirect + Induced Effects}}{\text{Direct Effects}}$$

Table 4B reports the summary multipliers for the six industries in the seven study communities. Interpolating the numbers from city A in Table 4B to the formula indicates that the personal income multiplier is 1.81:

$$\frac{.36 + .08 + .21}{.36} = \frac{.65}{.36} = 1.81$$

This multiplier indicates that for every $1 of personal income that accrues in the economy of city A, an additional 81 cents of indirect and induced income will be created. The size of the multiplier is determined by the relative size of the direct effect. A review of the data

in Tables 4A and 4B shows that large multipliers are indicative of direct effects coefficients that are small relative to the indirect and induced effects coefficients, while small multipliers have relatively large direct effects coefficients.

A consensus has emerged in the economic impact literature *that the multiplier coefficient indicator should be used rather than the multiplier measure* because it gives most guidance to policy makers. The multiplier merely indicates that if $1 of direct income is created, a proportion of additional personal income will be created in other parts of the economy. It does not give a meaningful indication of the impact on personal income, because it does not include information on size of the initial leakage. Because the multiplier is only a measure of internal linkage within an economy, to multiply it by visitor expenditures is meaningless. It is misleading, of no

Table 4B Summary **Multipliers** for the Six Industries on Which There Were Visitor Expenditures in the Seven Study Cities

City	Sales			Personal Income			Jobs		
	D	$\frac{(D+ID)}{D}$	$\frac{(D+ID+IDU)}{D}$	D	$\frac{(D+ID)}{D}$	$\frac{(D+ID+IDU)}{D}$	D	$\frac{(D+ID)}{D}$	$\frac{(D+ID+IDU)}{D}$
A	1.00	1.26	1.88	.36	1.23	1.81	27.71	1.13	1.52
B	1.00	1.28	2.29	.42	1.22	2.17	28.87	1.13	1.68
C	1.00	1.26	1.78	.37	1.24	1.77	25.53	1.13	1.44
D	1.00	1.29	2.41	.39	1.24	2.32	26.78	1.16	1.84
E	1.00	1.22	1.83	.38	1.19	1.74	22.11	1.13	1.53
F	1.00	1.29	2.12	.38	1.27	2.10	24.39	1.16	1.67
G	1.00	1.22	2.15	.40	1.19	2.08	22.78	1.12	1.71

D: Direct Effect   **ID**: Indirect Effect   **IDU**: Induced Effect

real value to policy makers, and should not be used. In contrast, multiplying the personal income coefficients by visitor expenditures generates a very meaningful number for policy makers. Almost two decades ago, one of the pioneers of economic impact analysis in this field advocated "general abandonment of the multiplier approach and consequent removal of the confusion which it creates. It is difficult to envisage how or why such an inappropriate approach has gained such wide usage. Unlike the multiplier coefficient, it has no basis in economic theory and it provides misleading policy prescription".[11]

In the case of the sales measure of economic impact, the direct effect is synonymous with the initial visitor expenditure injected into the economy. This means that the denominator is the same in calculations both of the multiplier coefficient and the multi-

plier. Hence, the sales measure remains the same, irrespective of whichever approach is used.

(e) Careful Interpretation of Employment Measures

An *employment* multiplier coefficient measures the direct, indirect and induced effect of an extra unit of visitor spending on employment in the host community. The employment multiplier reported in Table 4B shows that for every direct job visitor expenditures create in city A, an additional .52 jobs will be created elsewhere in the local economy. Again, the employment multipliers in Table 4B offer no guidance to policy makers, whereas the multiplier coefficients in Table 4A purport to show how many jobs are created in the community as a result of the visitor expenditure which may be useful information.

Employment coefficients are expressed in terms of number of jobs per million dollars in direct sales. Table 4A shows the summary employment coefficients for the six industries in the seven study communities in which the economic impact studies reported in this publication were undertaken. It indicates, for example, that in city A for every $1 million in indirect sales in these six industries by visitors from outside the area, about 28 direct jobs, 4 indirect jobs (31.36 - 27.71), and 11 induced jobs (42.07 - 31.36) for a total job impact of 42 jobs per million dollars of direct sales would be created.

There are three important caveats regarding the estimates of employment that should be noted. First, estimates include both full-time and part-time jobs, and do not distinguish between them. The employment measure does not identify the number of hours worked in each job, or the proportion of jobs which are full and part-time. However, it seems reasonable to posit that local businesses are unlikely to hire additional full-time employees in response to additional demands created by a tournament or event, because the extra business demand will last only for a few days. In these situations, the number of employees is not likely to increase. Rather, it is the number of hours that existing employees work that is likely to increase. Existing employees are likely to be requested to work overtime or to be released from other duties to accommodate this temporary peak demand. At best, only a few very short-term additional employees may be hired. Hence, it is improbable that anything like 42 jobs will be created in city A if an extra $1 million expenditures attributable to an event is forthcoming (Table 4A), and the few jobs that do emerge will probably be short-term, part-time jobs. However, decision-makers easily may be misled into assuming these are full-time positions.

Second, the employment estimates assume that all existing employees are fully occupied, so an increase in external visitor spending will require an increase in level of employment within the jurisdiction. In the context of the front desk of a hotel, for example, the employment estimator assumes that the existing staff would be unable to handle additional guests checking in for overnight stays associated with a tournament. However, in many cases, they are sufficiently underemployed to do this, so additional staff would not be needed. In these situations, the employment coefficient is exaggerated.

A third potentially misleading corollary of employment estimates is that they imply all new jobs will be filled by residents from within the community. However, it is possible that some proportion of them will be filled by commuters from outside the community. In these cases, it is inappropriate to conclude that all the jobs benefit the community's residents.

The first and second caveats suggest that the employment multiplier coefficient is an inappropriate output measure for reporting the economic impact of short term events such as festivals and sports tournaments. It becomes appropriate only when the focus is on park and recreation facilities, such as parks, golf courses, zoos, etc., where the durability of the enterprise suggests that jobs are likely to be full-time.

An Illustration of the Implications of Abusing the Basic Principles

The author was invited by a large American city to undertake a study that would assess the economic impact on the area of a 10 day festival which incorporated over 60 sports and cultural events. A multi-stage sampling procedure was used to collect data from over 2,600 festival participants. Data

Table 5 Economic Activity in City X Created by the Expenditures of Residents and Non-Residents Who Attended Festival Events

Items	Total Sales	Personal Income	Number of Jobs Created
Food & Beverage	109,196,634	48,238,234	3,110
Admission Fees	38,691,412	14,200,095	1,095
Night Clubs, Lounges & Bars	20,163,133	10,987,611	402
Retail Shopping	66,934,134	28,159,101	1,805
Lodging Expenses	47,872,258	19,922,456	1,148
Private Auto Expenses	14,727,339	5,123,586	259
Commercial Transportation	22,146,640	9,126,217	370
Other Expenses	1,874,950	1,076,825	69
TOTAL	321,606,500	136,834,125	8,258

from that study are used here to illustrate the egregious errors that occur when the central principles of economic impact studies described in the previous section are abused.

Because it was a large city with extensive suburbs, the defined area for which the economic impact study was undertaken was delineated as the county within which the city's boundaries were confined and two surrounding counties which embraced the city's suburbs. The three counties essentially represented the integrated local trading area. If the study had been limited to a single county, the economic interrelationships between city and suburbs would have been ignored and the results would have been less representative of economic impact on the area.

The data reported in Table 5 abuses four of the basic principles. The table reports "economic activity" not economic impact because it inappropriately includes local residents in the analysis; it prominently displays economic activity in terms of value of sales as well as in terms of personal income; it does not exclude time-switchers or casuals; and it displays total jobs created, failing to note that they are a combination of part-time and full-time jobs and that they are unlikely to be durable. From these results, the uninformed policymaker, media representative, or taxpayer may reasonably conclude that the economic impact of the festival was over $321 million and that it generated 8,258 full time jobs.

In Table 6 local residents' expenditures were removed from the analysis, so the table now reports economic impact and not economic activity. The aggregated impacts are substantially lower than those shown in Table 5, but they are still exaggerated because

Table 6   Economic Activity in City X of Expenditures by Non-Residents Who Attended Festival Events

Items	Total Sales	Personal Income	Number of Jobs Created*
Food & Beverage	37,859,887	16,737,554	1,078
Admission Fees	7,837,688	2,875,055	222
Night Clubs, Lounges & Bars	4,555,057	2,478,865	91
Retail Shopping	23,545,491	9,909,880	635
Lodging Expenses	35,124,109	14,637,961	843
Private Auto Expenses	4,744,930	1,653,118	84
Commercial Transportation	10,710,664	4,340,311	179
Other Expenses	1,088,768	458,243	29
TOTAL	125,466,594	53,090,987	3,161

* This figure refers to both full-time and part-time jobs. It assumes the local economy is operating at full capacity and that there is no slack to absorb additional demand created by these events

they include time-switchers and casuals. A footnote introduces appropriate caveats regarding the number of jobs created.

Respondents were asked questions which showed that 27% of non-local participants were time-switchers who would have visited the city if the festival had not been held, but the festival influenced their decision to come at that time. Another 43% were casuals who would have come to the city at that time, irrespective of the event. They went to the festival because it was an attractive entertainment option while they were in the community. Table 7 shows the impact on the city when these two groups were discarded from the analyses, because their expenditures would have entered the city's economy even if the event had not been held. In this survey,

time-switchers and casuals were not asked if their stay had been extended because of the festival. If there were extensions, then that increment of their expenditures should have been added to the total. To that extent, the economic impacts shown in Table 7 are underestimates.

The data shown in Table 7, excluding the sales column, were used in the presentation of the study's findings to the city's park and recreation board. The results were scheduled to be presented to the city council the following week. At the conclusion of the presentation, some board members quickly challenged the results arguing that they were much too low. They observed that two weeks previously, the city council had heard a similar presentation from the convention and

Table 7   Economic Activity in City X of Expenditures by Non-Residents (Excluding Casuals and Time Switchers) Who Attended Festival Events

Items	Total Sales	Personal Income	Number of Jobs Created*
Food & Beverage	7,371,629	5,088,151	328
Admission Fees	1,550,953	874,005	67
Night Clubs, Lounges & Bars	1,384,713	753,562	28
Retail Shopping	4,943,987	3,012,571	193
Lodging Expenses	6,655,528	4,449,879	256
Private Auto Expenses	824,220	502,541	25
Commercial Transportation	1,897,734	1,319,433	54
Other Expenses	213,126	139,305	9
TOTAL	24,841,890	16,139,447	960

* This figure refers to both full-time and part-time jobs. It assumes the local economy is operating at full capacity and that there is no slack to absorb additional demand created by these events

visitors bureau relating to a professional rodeo event that the city hosted annually. The council were informed that the economic impact of the 3 day professional rodeo event was almost $30 million. The conundrum confronting the park and recreation board was posed in the following terms:

How can we possibly accept that this festival lasting for 10 days and embracing over 60 events had a smaller economic impact than a single 3 day rodeo event? The city council provides a substantially larger budget to the parks and recreation department to stage the festival than they allocate to the convention and visitors bureau to host the professional rodeo event.

When they compare the festival data which has been presented to us with those from the rodeo there is a real possibility that the festival budget will be cut, because the festival costs much more to stage and its economic impact on the city is barely half that of the rodeo.

When a copy of the rodeo economic impact study was reviewed by the author, it was found that it abused four central principles--it included local residents; included time-switchers and casuals; used sales output as the measure of economic impact; and implied full-time jobs resulted from the visitors' expenditures. The author's response in his subsequent presentation to the city council was to replicate the presentation made to the park and recreation board, but then to extend it by referring to the rodeo study and showing that if those erroneous assumptions were applied to the festival the comparative number to the rodeo's almost $30 million was over $321 million (Table 5).

This illustration demonstrates the wide range of numbers which purport to measure economic impact that may be presented to stakeholders from the same set of primary data. If a press conference was held in city X to report the festival's economic impact, the organizers could, at one extreme, announce that the sales output from economic activity associated with the festival was over $321 million (Table 5). At the other extreme, they could announced that the economic impact of the festival on personal income was approximately $16 million (Table 7).

The media, general public, city council and other relevant publics are unlikely to be aware of the underlying assumptions, subtleties and potential error sources associated with economic impact studies. This lack of sophistication and the apparent objectively conveyed by the numbers, make it tempting for advocates to act unethically.

Clearly, there is a dilemma. If the correct $16 million figure for city X is presented, the festival's economic contribution is likely to appear relatively insignificant compared to other events which announce the equivalent of the $321 million figure as their estimated economic impact. The relatively small impact of the festival is likely to translate into commensurately less political and resource support for it from decision-makers, and perhaps, ultimately, even withdrawal of appropriations for it. Acting ethically when others do not, could critically damage the festival's standing.

Alternatively, some may rationalize that it is equitable to use the same set of measures to compare the economic contributions of

events, even though the results of all of them are grossly misleading. If such a position is accepted, then abuses incorporated into one economic impact analysis become contagious, because when precedent has been established in one study others are likely to feel compelled to knowingly perpetuate the abuse by incorporating the misleading procedures into their own analyses. If they fail to do so, then the economic impact attributed to their event or facility is perceived to be lower than that reported by others and thus less worthy of public investment.

Continued abuse of economic impact principles by advocates inevitably will lead to the technique being discounted by decision-makers. The author adhered to the central principles in his presentation to the council. But at the same time, it was necessary to recognize the political reality of being compared to others who had reported misleading economic impacts to the park and recreation agency's legislative body. The conundrum was resolved during the presentation by identifying the erroneous assumptions which the rodeo event incorporated and demonstrating how the festival study's results would be inflated if the same erroneous assumptions were incorporated into it.

Consideration of Costs

The numbers emerging from an economic impact study represent only the gross economic benefits associated with an event. Too often, only positive economic benefits associated with visitors are reported, and costs of negative impacts inflicted on a community are not considered. Community stakeholders are likely to be more concerned with net, rather than gross, economic benefits. This involves identifying the costs associated with an event and deducting their economic value from the positive economic impacts shown by an analysis. Clearly, if costs exceed the benefits then, even if there is a relatively high gross economic impact, the event may not be a good investment for the community.

Incorporating costs into a study changes it from an economic impact analysis to a benefit-cost analysis. In the author's view, decision-makers should be attempting to use benefit-cost analysis when evaluating alternative investments, despite the difficulties associated with deriving accurate costs. Three types of costs should be considered: (a) infrastructure costs; (b) displacement costs; and (c) opportunity costs.

Infrastructure Costs

Infrastructure costs may be both on-site and off-site. On-site costs include the cost of additional equipment or supplies; the cost of additional labor contracted by an agency to assist with an event; and cost of the time invested in the project by the agency's existing employees. In Table 2, for example, the labor and equipment costs incurred by the city parks and recreation department in hosting a softball tournament were tracked, recorded and included in the analysis, so the economic impact net of on-site infrastructure costs could be presented.

When large numbers of visitors are attracted to a community, they are likely to create extra demands on its services and inflict social costs on community residents. Off-site infrastructure costs borne by the community as a result of an event may include such items as traffic congestion, road accidents, vandalism, police and fire protection, environmental degradation, garbage collection, increased prices to local residents in retail and restaurant establishments, loss of access, and disruption of residents' lifestyles. Translating some of these impacts into economic values is relatively easy (for example, costs of extra police or fire protection and

off-site clean-up costs), but in other cases it is difficult which is one reason why they are usually ignored. If some of these costs cannot be translated into economic values, they should at least be described, qualitatively assessed and included in a presentation to a legislative body, so they are considered in an evaluation of an event's net benefits. An alternative approach is to monitor the level of residents' tolerance to these off-site costs during the event, and questionnaire instruments for this purpose have been developed.[12]

Displacement Costs

There is some likelihood that visitors from outside a community who are attracted by a park and recreation agency event, may displace other visitors who otherwise would have come to the community but do not, either because they cannot obtain accommodations or because they are not prepared to mingle with crowds attracted by the event.

While the scale of a parks and recreation event would obviously be much smaller, the displacement cost principle was illustrated by an economic impact study done on the Los Angeles Olympic Games. The study estimated that $163 million of out-of-region visitor expenditures did not occur in Southern California during the period of the Games which would have accrued if they had not been held.[13] Hence, this amount was deducted from the gross economic impact in order to arrive at the event's net economic impact.

The displacement amount was attributed to two factors. First, widespread national media reporting of potential congestion at the Olympic Games, and of exorbitant pricing by motels and hotels, negatively affected potential tourists and visitors. Second, the Olympic Games had been scheduled for Los Angeles for six years, so alternative vacation visitation and business trip plans were made by potential out-of-town tourists, by regional residents, and by businesses.

Opportunity Costs

For an investment of public money to be justified, it must meet the criterion of "highest and best use." That is, it should yield a return to residents that is at least equal to that which could be obtained from other ventures in which the government entity could invest. Opportunity cost is the value of the best alternative not taken when a decision to expend government money is made.

A positive net economic impact does not mean that a park and recreation tournament or event necessarily should be supported, because the opportunity cost associated with this investment may be unacceptably high. If, for example, an alternative project has a higher net economic impact, presumably it has a stronger case for support.

Figure 3 showed that money used to create park and recreation events has been contributed by community residents in the form of taxes. This represents an opportunity cost because residents are likely to have spent those funds in the community if the government had not taken them. In essence, the government may be perceived as spending it for them, so the net gain to the community is zero. The process merely substitutes public expenditures for private expenditures, and the resources allocated to a park and recreation event are denied to other sectors of the economy. This point has been articulated in the following terms:

> While governments may like to believe that their contributions are "productive," unless total receipts from outside the region are increased by the government financing contribution, all that is happening is that public funding is being substituted for private funding and there is no net economic benefit to the State--just a public cost.[14]

Expenditures by local governments are costs because they are financed by residents within the host community who therefore have to forego something else, and there is no extra generation of income. Thus, an expenditure on park and recreation events by a local government cannot be considered an injection of new funds. If resources are injected into an economy from non-local governments, they can be considered as new money only if they would not have come to the community without the project. Thus, federal funds such as Community Development Block Grants, which are awarded to communities on a formula basis and have been used in some communities to fund park and recreation services, should not be included in economic impact analyses because they could legitimately have been allocated to a variety of alternative community projects.

CHAPTER 3

DATA COLLECTION AND ANALYSIS PROCEDURES

The Design and Content of the Questionnaire

A sample questionnaire for collecting the information needed to calculate economic impact is shown in Figure 5. A major goal was that the questionnaire should be short. The shorter it is, the less time it takes respondents to complete, and the more likely it is that they will cooperate in the study. To achieve this goal, it was imperative that the questionnaire should contain only essential questions. The criterion used in developing it was, "What will be done with the information from this question?" Questions which may have produced "interesting information" were not included unless that information was essential for calculating economic impact. In this section, the rationale supporting each question on the questionnaire shown in Figure 5 is explained.

> 1. What is the zip code at your home address?

This question is designed to differentiate between local and non-local respondents. In chapter 2, it was pointed out that economic impact refers only to expenditures made by out-of-town visitors, so those who live locally must be screened out and eliminated from the study's calculations. If respondents report that they are local residents, then there is no point in them completing any more of the questionnaire, since the information they provide will not be used.

However, if the response to question 1 indicates that a respondent group is comprised of local residents, this contact should not merely be disregarded. *The contact with them must be recorded even though they do not complete the remaining questions, because this information is essential for calculating the proportion of visitors who are from out-of-town.* For example, if 1000 individuals are sampled and 600 of them are local residents, then it is concluded that only 40% of visitors to the event came from out-of-town. If the total event attendance is 200,000, then this information suggests that 80,000 are from out-of-town. This is the attendance number of interest in economic impact studies (not the 200,000 figure), and the number to which results provided by the sample are extrapolated.

Zip codes enable "the local area" to be configured in any way the study sponsor desires. Thus, local catchment area may be defined as selected areas of a city; by a city's

1. What is the zip code at your home address? _____

2. Which of the following days will you be at this event? (Please circle **_all_** that apply)

    <u>Friday</u>   <u>Saturday</u>   <u>Sunday</u>

3. How many people (**<u>including yourself</u>**) are in your immediate group? (This is the number of people for whom you typically pay the bills. e.g., your family or close friends) _____ people

---

Alternative questions 1 and 2 to be used (question 3 is omitted) in the context of a sports tournament

1. What is the name of your team? _____

2. How many players are there on your team at this tournament? _____

---

4. To better understand the economic impact of the (Name of Event), we are interested in finding out the approximate amount of money you and other visitors in your immediate group will spend, including travel to and from your home. We understand that this is a difficult question, but please do your best because your responses are very important to our efforts. **DURING THE COURSE OF YOUR VISIT, WHAT IS THE APPROXIMATE AMOUNT <u>YOUR IMMEDIATE GROUP</u> WILL SPEND IN EACH OF THE FOLLOWING CATEGORIES**:

TYPE OF EXPENDITURE	Amount spent in the (name of city) area	Amount spent Outside the (name of city) area
A. Admission / Entry Fees	_____	_____
B. Food & Beverages (restaurants, concessions, grocery stores, etc.)	_____	_____
C. Entertainment, Lounges & Bars (cover charges, drinks, etc.)	_____	_____
D. Retail Shopping (clothing, souvenirs, gifts, etc.)	_____	_____
E. Lodging Expenses (hotel, motel, etc.)	_____	_____
F. Private Auto Expenses (gas, oil, repairs, parking fees, etc.)	_____	_____
G Rental Car Expenses	_____	_____
H. Any Other Expenses	_____	_____

Please identify: _____

Questions 5 and 6 are not required for sports tournaments.

5. Would you have come to the (Name of City) area <u>at this time</u> even if this event had not been held?

    Yes_____   No_____

    5a. If "Yes", did you stay longer in the (Name of City) area than you would have done if this event had not been held?

    Yes_____   No_____

    5b. If "Yes" (<u>in 5a</u>), how much longer? _____Days

6. Would you have come to (Name of City) in the next three months if you had not come at this time for this event?

    Yes_____   No_____

Figure 5. Economic Impact Questionnaire

boundaries; by a city and its suburbs; by a county; or whatever. Indeed, zip codes enable the economic impact of an event or facility on each of these different catchment areas to be calculated if sponsors wish to do this, since it is easy for the computer to aggregate zip codes into any desired configurations.

> 2. Which of the following days will you be at this event? (Please circle **_all_** that apply)
>
> Friday   Saturday   Sunday

Obviously, if the event of interest was scheduled for only one day, then this question would be omitted. Responses to this question enable both per day per person and per day per visitor group economic impact data to be calculated. Examples of these calculations are given in chapter 4. This permits agencies to compare the economic impacts of events which have different timeframes to ascertain what types of events offer best return to a community for the resources it invests. The per day data also enable the results from events that are surveyed to be extrapolated easily to other similar events that may be of different duration and at which no surveying is undertaken.

> 3. How many people **(including yourself)** are in your immediate group? (This is the number of people for whom you typically pay the bills. e.g., your family or close friends) _____ people

This question is designed to direct respondents' thinking towards the immediate group which is the unit of analysis used in the next question that collects the financial information. The question also permits per person and per visitor group expenditures to

be calculated which facilitate comparisons across an agency's events and extrapolation to non-surveyed events.

Knowledge of the group size is essential in special event contexts because total expenditures are calculated by multiplying the sample responses up to the total attendance. This is illustrated in the following calculation:

Total number of event visitors from out-of-town	15000
Average expenditure per respondent's immediate group	$30
Average size of immediate group	3

Total expenditures by out-of-town visitors to the event are

$$\frac{15,000}{3} \times \$30 = \$150,000$$

This calculation could not be made without knowing the group size. Group size is not needed in studies involving team sports because the team rather than the individual is the unit of analysis.

> Alternative questions 1 and 2 to be used (question 3 is omitted) in the context of a sports tournament.
>
> 1. What is the name of your team?
>
> _____
>
> 2. How many players are there on your team at this tournament?
>
> _____

Data at sports tournaments are collected by randomly selecting a limited number of teams in the tournament, and then surveying all (or as many as possible) of the players on the selected teams' squads. This procedure requires that both a participant's team name and the number of players on that team's squad be requested on the questionnaire. At the same time, players' or teams' zip codes are not required, since tournament organizers can provide information on which teams are local and which are from out-of-town. The days of a sports tournament are fixed, so question 2 is redundant. Similarly, since total participation is measured by teams and not individuals and the aggregate number of teams in a tournament is known by the organizers, question 3 is not needed. However, if question 3 is omitted, then the definition of immediate group which is shown in parenthesis in question 3 will need to be included in question 4. Thus, questions 1, 2 and 3 described in previous paragraphs are replaced by the above alternative two questions in the context of a sports tournament:

It would be inaccurate to capture only the expenditures of individual respondents be-

cause they may be paying for other people or, alternatively, others may be paying for them. The only way to avoid these error sources is to capture the expenditures of all members of the immediate group. Thus, the immediate group is emphasized in question 4 which is shown below.

It was noted in chapter 2 that each category of expenditure has a different multiplier coefficient, so expenditures have to be identified by category. Experience has shown that nearly all out-of-town visitor expenditures associated with park and recreation events fall into the first seven categories shown in question 4. If there is no admission charge or entry fee, then category A should be omitted. If expenditures are assigned to category H, it is important to specify what they were for, so they are assigned to the correct industrial sector in the multiplier model.

In sports tournaments, the entry fee category usually may be omitted because it is

---

4. To better understand the economic impact of the (Name of Event), we are interested in finding out the approximate amount of money you and other visitors in your immediate group will spend, including travel to and from your home. We understand that this is a difficult question, but please do your best because your responses are very important to our efforts. **DURING THE COURSE OF YOUR VISIT, WHAT IS THE APPROXIMATE AMOUNT <u>YOUR IMMEDIATE GROUP</u> WILL SPEND IN EACH OF THE FOLLOWING CATEGORIES:**

TYPE OF EXPENDITURE	Amount spent in the (name of city) area	Amount spent outside the (name of city) area
A. Admission / Entry Fees	_____	_____
B. Food & Beverages (restaurants, concessions, grocery stores, etc.)	_____	_____
C. Entertainment, Lounges & Bars (cover charges, drinks, etc.)	_____	_____
D. Retail Shopping (clothing, souvenirs, gifts, etc.)	_____	_____
E. Lodging Expenses (hotel, motel, etc.)	_____	_____
F. Private Auto Expenses (gas, oil, repairs, parking fees, etc.)	_____	_____
G. Rental Car Expenses	_____	_____
H. Any Other Expenses	_____	_____

Please identify: _____

sent to the organizers in one payment on behalf of all team members. Hence, the amount is known and does not have to be ascertained from information provided by individual players. Also, each team's coach/captain should be asked if any of the team's local expenditures are being directly paid by sponsors (e.g. accommodation or meals). In such cases, these amounts should be added to the data collected from individual players' questionnaires and included in calculations of teams' total expenditures.

Question 4 requires respondents to give their expenditures both within the area of interest and outside that area. Economic impact studies are concerned only with the amount of money spent in the area of interest, so the information reported in the second column pertaining to expenditures outside the area is discarded. Even though it is not used, this information is requested because it causes respondents to think carefully about where they spent their money. If it were omitted, there is a greater probability of respondents not reading the question carefully and incorrectly attributing all their trip expenditures to the host area.

Ideally, the headings on column one in this question would be defined by zip code, viz, "Amount spent in the following zip codes:____". This would ensure that the reported expenditures coincided with the selected configuration of the impacted area which is defined by zip codes. Unfortunately, most people, residents as well as visitors, are unlikely to know the boundaries of zip code areas so a surrogate descriptor (usually the city or neighborhood name) has to be selected that respondents will recognize.

The expenditures reported in question 4 can only be approximations because (1) if respondents complete the questionnaire before they leave the event and the impacted area, they have to estimate the additional expenditures they are likely to incur; and (2) if they

complete the questionnaire after the event and mail it back, then their recall memory may be faulty. This reinforces the realization that economic impact studies can only be "guesstimates."

Questions 5 and 6 are designed to identify time-switchers and casuals. These questions are not likely to be relevant in the context of sports tournaments because spontaneous, casual participation in such events is not possible and experience has shown that the proportion of players who planned to come to the community at another time is negligible. Thus, the questionnaire used in the economic impact studies of sports tournaments consists only of three questions and the latter two are omitted.

5. Would you have to come to the (Name of City) area at this time even it this event had not been held?

    Yes _____   No _____

5a. If "Yes", did you stay longer in the (Name of City) area than you would have done if this event had not been held?

    Yes _____   No _____

5b. If "Yes" (in 5a.), how much longer?

    _____ Days

Those who answer "yes" to question 5 are classified as casuals and are omitted from the study, unless they also answer "yes" to question 5a. These individuals were already in the community, but were attracted there by other factors. Their economic impact cannot be attributed to the event because it was not responsible for bringing them to the community, and if they had not elected to attend then it is likely they would have spent their money somewhere else in the community. However, if the event causes them to stay in the jurisdiction for more days than they would have done if the event had not been held, then their incremental expenditures on those extra days should be included in the economic impact analysis. This information is captured in questions 5a and 5b.

6. Would you have come to (Name of City) in the next three months if you had not at this time for this event?

Yes _____   No _____

Question 6 is designed to identify time-switchers. Those who respond "yes" changed the timing of an intended visit to the community to coincide with the event. They will be omitted from the analysis because their spending in the community cannot be attributed to the event since it would have occurred without the event, albeit at a different time of the year.

The results reported in chapter 4 refer only to the economic impact of participants or visitors at the events. They do not include economic impact derived from the expenditures of other groups associated with the events such as professional athletes or entertainers, vendors, media personnel and coaches. If these groups are involved and their economic contributions are to be estimated, then each of them needs to be sampled because it is likely that different groups will report different expenditure amounts and patterns. This would require an additional item which would appear at the beginning of the questionnaire:

Which of the following are you?

Spectator   Coach   Athlete

Media person   Vendor

Other _____

How Should the Data Be Collected?

Data can be collected either through the mail, or by interviewers on-site. In cases where a list of out-of-town visitors' addresses is available, for example, a triathlon event or sports tournament where individual participants have to register, the questionnaire may be sent to a sample of respondents through the mail. It should be accompanied by a cover letter briefly explaining the survey's purpose, and a stamped self-addressed envelope should be enclosed for respondents to return the completed survey to the agency.

Since they complete the questionnaire back in their home after the event, all expenses are known and respondents are not required to estimate any of them. This is a relatively inexpensive method of collecting data and it enables visitors to reflect on the questions at their leisure before answering them. The major disadvantage is that the number who return the questionnaire may be rather low. To attain the desired response rate of at least 70%, it is likely to require two follow-up letters enclosing a duplicate questionnaire to those who don't respond to the initial letter. These should be mailed out to non-respondents two weeks and four weeks after the original questionnaire is mailed.

A variation of this approach that can be used at events where addresses of out-of-town visitors are not available is to hand to selected respondents on-site a questionnaire with a cover letter and pre-paid return envelope. Those selected are informed of the study's purpose and a commitment is sought from them to complete the questionnaire and return it within a given period. This advanced commitment and the personal contact usually lead to a substantially higher proportion of questionnaires being returned than is achieved by mailing the questionnaire to them without any prior contact. However, respondents' names and addresses are recorded when they commit to cooperating, so follow-ups can be mailed if their completed questionnaire is not received in the following 10 days or so.

A third data collection alternative is to collect the information from out-of-town visitors while they are on-site. One way of doing this is to include the survey in all participants' registration packages or in event programs. Unfortunately, this usually results in unacceptably low response rates, as few people bother to complete them. However, the approach can be successful if it is reinforced with repeated exhortations over a public address system and substantial incentives are provided. For example, the author collected data at a Houston Astros baseball game by including a survey in the program. A sponsor provided four deluxe television sets that were offered as prizes in a drawing. Entry was a completed survey. Spectators were required to put their completed questionnaires into one of the collection boxes located at multiple points in each section. These were supervised by the stewards. After the fifth innings, stewards took the boxes to a central collection point on the field. The drawing was held during the seventh innings stretch. Completed questionnaires were received from over 17,000 of the 31,000 fans attending the game!

A more common on-site approach, which was adopted in all the studies reported in chapter 4, is to hand visitors a questionnaire on a clipboard with a pen, and wait while they complete it. There are two disadvantages associated with on-site data collection. First, respondents are unlikely to be in the contemplative mind-set which leads to careful answers, because of the immediate excitement of the event environment. Second, some of their expenditures have to be projected estimates, because respondents' on-site experiences are not complete and the off-site expenditures on their return home have

not yet been incurred. There is some evidence which suggests that on-site surveys typically underestimate expenditure projections. In the context of sports tournaments the underestimation has been explained in the following terms:

> Expenditures often depend on the outcome of a competition and if the subject's team or favorite athlete wins or loses. Early elimination may cause a spectator or participant to leave the impact area early and reduce expenditures, or a positive outcome may encourage the spectator and participant/team to celebrate out on the town thus increasing expenditures. The weather could also have an impact as to the length of time fans stay in the area.[15]

In all of the 30 studies reported in chapter 4, data were collected on-site. At only one of them was an address list of out-of-town visitors available. Thus, in 29 cases the first alternative of mailing out questionnaires was not a viable option. The second alternative of handing out questionnaires on site and requesting they be mailed back to the agency was rejected because of the shortness of the questionnaire. This alternative required respondents to write down their names and addresses to facilitate follow-ups which takes a minute or so, while completing the questionnaire itself took less than two minutes. Hence, this approach was deemed to be relatively inefficient. Further, collecting the completed questionnaires relieved agencies of the expense of organizing and mailing follow-ups to non-respondents.

Incentives are often used to encourage people to cooperate. If either of the first two alternative approaches are adopted, which required the sample to mail back completed questionnaires, then the most typical incentive is a drawing for prizes contributed by event sponsors or by the organizing agency. Entry for the drawing is a completed returned questionnaire. If data are collected on site, then couponing is the most common incentive. In return for completing the questionnaire, respondents are given a coupon which can be exchanged for a free beverage or free admission to one of the event's attractions.

How Many People Should Be Sampled?

After the questionnaire has been developed, the next issue to consider is, "To how many people should it be distributed?" The goal is to survey as few people as are necessary to secure accurate results.

Large numbers are not likely to be required. The minimum size sample of out-of-town visitors will vary according to the precision level the agency seeks, and the method used to select respondents. It is incorrect to assume that a substantially larger sample is needed for larger events. Provided the number of out-of-town visitors to an event is not extremely small, size will have little impact upon the number of responses required to achieve reasonable precision. This may be explained by the following illustration:

Suppose a barrel is filled with 10,000 marbles, half red and half white. From this barrel a sample of 400 marbles is drawn, and it is found that the sample is divided 50-50. A very similar sample result would probably occur if the 400 marbles were taken from a barrel containing 20,000 red and white marbles or one containing 200,000 red and white marbles.

Table 8 shows the general relationship between sample size and level of accuracy for different sized events, if a random sampling procedure is used. The table suggests that for an event with 3000 out-of-town visitors, a sample of 353 will give results accurate to within plus or minus five percent, whereas an event with 500,000 out-of-town visitors requires a sample of only 400 (that is 47 more respondents) to give results that also are accurate to within plus or minus five percent.

An error of ± five percent means that if 50 percent of those surveyed say they would have visited a community in the next three months if they had not come at this time for this event, then the "true" percentage could be as low as 45 percent or as high as 55 percent if all out-of-town visitors to the event had been surveyed. It is important to recognize that this five percent error limit refers to a maximum *absolute* percentage error. For example, if 20 percent responded affirmatively to this question and a five percent error limit was used, the maximum range of tolerance is from 15 percent to 25 percent.

The smaller the error range, the more reliable the survey results. It is likely that an error range of 5 percent will be acceptable to most park and recreation agencies, which means that a sample of only a few hundred out-of-town visitors may be used to calculate the total economic impact, *if the sample is randomly selected*.

The numbers discussed in this section refer to out-of-town visitors. It was noted in the previous section of this chapter that the sample is most likely to be selected from on-site visitors because lists of visitors' addresses needed for mail surveys generally are not available. Typically, in an on-site survey there is no way to differentiate between local residents and out-of-town visitors until they respond to question 1. Thus, if only 25% of 50,000 visitors to an event are from out-of-town then even if all of those approached agree to cooperate, it is likely that 1588 (4 x

Table 8 Number of Out-of-Town Visitors to be Sampled to Deliver a Given Level of Accuracy, Assuming a Randomly Selected Sample

Number of Out-of-Town Participants or Visitors	Percentage Error Rate (Plus or Minus)				
	1%	2%	3%	4%	5%
1,000	*	*	*	385	286
2,000	*	*	714	476	333
3,000	*	1,364	811	517	353
4,000	*	1,538	870	541	364
5,000	*	1,667	909	556	370
10,000	5,000	2,000	1,000	588	385
20,000	6,667	2,222	1,053	606	392
25,000	7,143	2,273	1,064	610	394
50,000	8,333	2,381	1,087	617	397
100,000	9,091	2,439	1,099	621	398
500,000	9,804	2,488	1,101	625	400

* In these cases more than 50 percent of the visitors from out-of-town are required in the sample.

397) people will have to be contacted in order to get 397 questionnaires completed from out-of-town visitors.

Sampling Methods

Sampling methods for selecting respondents are classified as either probability or non-probability methods. Figure 6 summarizes the most common probability and non-probability sampling methods used to collect economic impact data. The major distinction between the two categories is that in a probability sample each out-of-town visitor to the event has a reasonably equal chance (probability) of being selected for the sample. Probability samples should be used whenever they are practical for two reasons. First, they eliminate bias which could occur in selecting

the sample respondents. Second, the recommended sample sizes shown in Table 8 assume that a simple random sample is being used.

Probability Sampling

It might be impossible to strictly apply probability sampling designs in the context of on-site surveys. However, it is desirable to adopt the principles of these sampling designs to the greatest extent possible in order to reduce sampling bias.

There are four types of probability samples. In a ***random sample*** all visitors have an equal chance of being chosen. This is done by using a set of random numbers to select respondents from a list of everybody visiting the site. This method is rarely feasible in on-site event situations, but it may be possible at some spectator events. For example, if a seating plan of a stadium, arena or theater is available in advance, then each seat can be numbered. A computer generated set of random numbers can be used to select the seats to be sampled. Interviewers then access those in the selected seats and request them to complete the questionnaire. However, even in these contexts, the practical difficulties associated with interviewers accessing those seated in the middle of rows makes random sampling difficult to implement.

A *stratified sample* is used when proportionate representation is sought from various segments of visitors. This method entails dividing visitors into groups or strata based upon a characteristic. In economic impact studies the characteristics most frequently used to stratify a sample are types of visitors, entrances to the site or time of day.

Types of visitors refer to different sub-groups such as spectators, athletes, entertainers, vendors and media personnel. If it is anticipated that their expenditure patterns in the community are likely to differ significantly, then it is desirable to sample a number from each sub-group that accurately reflects the sub-group's proportion of all visitors to the event.

At large event sites which have controlled gated areas, accuracy may be increased if the sample is selected in proportion to the number of people who pass through each gate. This becomes important if for some reason different kinds of people enter at different gates. This may occur, for example, if the main car park is close to one gate, a parking area for charter buses close to another, and public transport access points are near to a third. In such cases, stratifying a sample makes it more likely that the proportionality

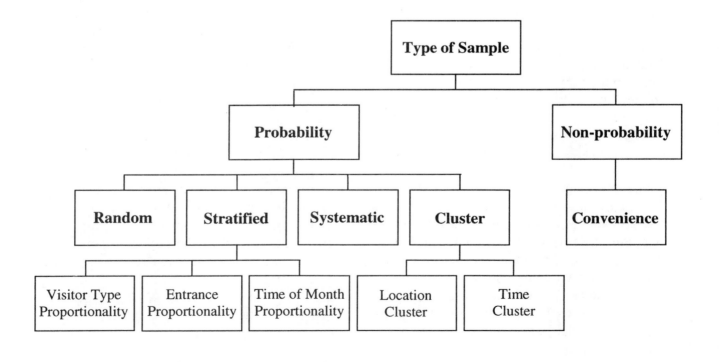

Figure 6. Alternative Sampling Methods

of all visitors would be reflected in the sample. Thus, if there were three gates and the proportions of visitors entering the grounds through them were 60%, 30% and 10%, then the sample would be structured so the proportion of respondents interviewed at each gate would reflect this ratio. This is accomplished by employing probability proportionate to size (PPS) sampling. PPS sampling is based on the percentage of visitors in each stratum. Thus, if 60 %of visitors used a specific gate, then 60 % of the total sample should be selected from those entering at that gate.

Stratifying may also improve accuracy if the profile of visitors is likely to differ by time of day or day of the week. For example, at a three day event, if 80% came on a Saturday and only 20% on Thursday and Friday, this ratio should be reflected in the sample by interviewing 80% of the total sample on the Saturday. The expenditures of Saturday visitors may be different from those who come on Thursday and Friday. They may have come from further afield than the Thursday and Friday visitors, because they were unencumbered by work commitments on the Saturday. Consequently, more of them may stay overnight in the community and spend more money there. Failure to reflect this ratio in the sampling plan may lead to a significant underestimate of the event's economic impact.

The most common form of probability sampling used in economic impact studies is *systematic sampling*. This involves selecting every n[th] person (every 5th, 20th, 28th or whatever) who enters or leaves the site. This is feasible only at events that have controlled access points and cannot work in contexts where the site is unfenced and people can enter indiscriminantly from anywhere on the perimeter.

Cluster sampling is similar to stratified sampling in that visitors are divided into sev-

eral groups or clusters. In this design, however, each sampling unit is a group or cluster of visitors. Cluster sampling involves two stages. First, some of groups or clusters are selected randomly and, second, samples are drawn from these clusters. This method might be efficient when the characteristics of visitors are fairly homogeneous across the clusters. For example, if there are 10 entrances to a site and there is no reason to assume that visitors at each entrance are different, there is no need to conduct interviews at every entry point. Visitors through each entrance may be regarded as a cluster, and a small number of entrances can be randomly selected as survey points. The desired sample number then can be selected at these points using a random or systematic approach.

If the data are collected on-site, it is usual to do it as visitors enter the site. The disadvantage of this strategy is that visitors are required to estimate their projected expenditures in the local community for the rest of their stay. For this reason, conceptually, the preferred approach would appear to be to interview people as they leave the site. However, experience has shown this is difficult for two reasons. First, people typically are less patient and less willing to cooperate at the end of their experience than at the beginning. Second, there are often logistical challenges because egress from a site often is more concentrated than access to it. People often filter into a festival site over a 3 or 4 hour time period, but they may all leave together at the end of the day. Similarly, at a ball game they may drift in over a 1 or 2 hour period before the game, but when it ends there is a mass exodus. These conditions make it difficult to interview the desired number of respondents.

Non-probability Sampling

Although probability sampling methods

are preferred because they ensure more accurate representation, there are many situations in which such methods are not feasible. Common examples are events located at sites that have an open perimeter without controlled access and egress points. In these contexts, there are no alternatives to using a non-probability, *convenience* sample. As the name implies, a convenience sample is selected on the basis of convenience or accessibility.

Visitors are intercepted by interviewers at points around the site. An effort should be made to introduce as much randomness as possible into the process by instructing interviewers to intercept every n^{th} person passing them. Nevertheless, there are some visitors who may never pass an interviewer point while others may pass multiple interviewer points on multiple occasions, so visitors' chances of being selected for the sample are not equal and are not known. Thus, the survey's results may be unrepresentative, and this has to be accepted as a limitation of the study.

It is important to conduct a training session for interviewers before the event. At this session, they should be instructed on such issues as how to select respondents, how to approach them, and how to administer the survey. A training guide is provided in Appendix 2.

Using and Interpreting IMPLAN

In the past, it was not feasible for local agency managers to calculate with reasonable accuracy the multiplier effect of visitor expenditures in a community. To do this, trained economists had to be hired to construct an input-output model which could examine relationships within the local economy both between businesses, and between businesses and final consumers. This requires the collection of large amounts of data from local industries and is a complex, laborious and expensive process. Thus, the only recourse to agencies wanting to incorporate an indicator of the multiplier effect was to use an arbitrary coefficient that purported to be "conventional wisdom." Such "guesstimates" had no empirical basis and often were unreasonably high because they were promulgated by tourism or economic development advocates.

In recent years, this situation has changed with the widespread availability of IMPLAN which was developed as a cost-effective means of producing local input-output models. Instead of building input-output models with primary data collected directly from local industries, IMPLAN is an input-output modeling system that builds its accounts with secondary data collected from a multitude of federal government agencies that was originally collected for other purposes.

IMPLAN is derived from IMpact analysis for PLANing. The original developmental work on it was initiated in 1979 by the USDA Forest Service's Land Management Unit in Fort Collins, Colorado, in cooperation with the Federal Emergency Management Agency and the USDI Bureau of Land Management, to assist the Forest Service in land and resource management planning. They subsequently linked with the University of Minnesota. However, in 1993 IMPLAN transitioned from the public sector to the private sector in order to facilitate continued development of the data bases and analytical tools. The system is now owned by the Minnesota IMPLAN Group, Inc.

There are two components to the IMPLAN system, the software and the data bases. The software performs the calculations and is available for personal computers using a Windows format. The data bases are updated annually and provide all the information needed to create the IMPLAN input-output models. They provide information from 528 different industrial sectors, closely following the accounting conventions used by the U.S. Bureau of Economic Analysis. The data bases incorporate comprehensive data for the entire United States. They are available in standard form at the county, state or U.S. level, and can also be customized and made available at the zip code level. Thus, an input-output model can be defined for a section of a city, a single city, a single county, several counties, a state, a group of states, or the entire United States.

The areas on which the studies reported in the next chapter were conducted were defined by zip code, because the cooperating communities wanted results that related specifically to their city boundaries rather than to the broader county boundaries. The use of zip codes to define a study area smaller than a county is likely to lead to some overstatement of the induced effects, because it is derived by a proportional reduction of a larger database. This assumes that employees live within the zip code area in the same proportions as in the larger database. The smaller the area, the less likely this is true, and this

Table 9 Cost of IMPLAN State Data Packages

State	Cost	State	Cost	State	Cost	State	Cost
AK	$1,100	ID	$1,350	MT	$1,450	RI	$525
AL	$1,450	IL	$1,800	NC	$1,775	SC	$1,325
AR	$1,475	IN	$1,650	ND	$1,450	SD	$1,450
AZ	$775	KS	$1,750	NE	$1,675	TN	$1,700
CA	$1,450	KY	$1,950	NH	$725	TX	$2,200
CO	$1,450	LA	$1,450	NJ	$950	UT	$1,125
CT	$725	MA	$750	NM	$1,150	VA	$2,000
DC	$300	MD	$1,000	NY	$1,450	VT	$750
DE	$475	ME	$800	NV	$825	WA	$1,150
FL	$1,450	MI	$1,700	OH	$1,675	WI	$1,475
GA	$2,150	MN	$1,675	OK	$1,475	WV	$1,450
HI	$500	MO	$1,875	OR	$1,150	WY	$1,000
IA	$1,750	MS	$1,675	PA	$1,450		

Individual County File	$150
US or State Totals File	$300
Zip Code Level Files	$350

causes the induced effects to be overstated.

To run a local economic analysis, both the statewide and local county or zip code input-output models and databases are needed. The current cost of purchasing these can be found on the IMPLAN web site, which is www.IMPLAN.com. The costs that prevailed when this publication was written are shown in Table 9. The cost of purchasing software and data bases for the three zip codes which define the city of College Station, Texas, at the rates shown in Table 9, would be $350. If concern was with the economic impact on Brazos County, which is the county in which College Station is located, then the $350 city cost would be replaced by the $150 county cost. If the impact on both entities was required then the cost would be $500. The package for Texas costs $2,200 (Table 9) and includes data for every county in the State. An individual trained in the use of IMPLAN can produce the economic impact measures in a few hours once the expenditure data have been entered into the model.

Three types of multipliers are recognized. Type I measures direct effect plus indirect effect divided by the direct effect. It captures the inter-industry effects only, that is, industries buying from local industries. Thus, it includes only the original expenditures resulting from the impacts plus the indirect effects of industries buying from industries. Household expenditures effect, that is, the induced effects, are not estimated. Type II and Type III multipliers include induced effects in the numerator along with direct and indirect effects. Although they use the same formulas, the data for Type II and Type III multipliers are calculated differently, and the IMPLAN manual advises, "Unless you have specific reasons not to, we suggest using the software's Type II multipliers."[16]

IMPLAN calculates eight different measures of economic impact, but only four of these are commonly used. They are sales, personal income, value added, and employment. These were defined in chapter 2 where it was noted that the most appropriate of these are either the personal income or the value added measures, since they best fit the conceptual rationale for undertaking economic impact studies that was described in Figure 3.

CHAPTER 4

RESULTS OF 30 ECONOMIC IMPACT STUDIES

The National Recreation and Park Association solicited cities to participate in a study of the economic impact of sports tournaments and special events that were organized by park and recreation agencies. The study's goal was to collect reasonably accurate data from a substantial number of events, and to estimate the economic impacts of these events which would be free from the types of common errors and abuses described in chapter 2. It was anticipated that reviewing the results from a relatively large number of case studies may reveal some consistent patterns of expenditures.

Researchers will be quick to point out that results from the tournaments and events in the seven cities reported here are likely to differ from those obtained by studies done on similar events in other communities, because the contexts are likely to be different:

Unique factors include the geographic proximity of the participating teams to the host site, novelty of the destination for spectators and participants, the size of the sport venue, the location of the sport venue to the business district, the level of supporting infrastructure in the host community, changes in the format of the event (e.g. amount of rest between matches) and time between qualifying tournaments and the championship tournament. The shorter the time, the less opportunity for sport tourists to plan their trips. The amount of positive or negative media attention, promotional budget, weather and accessibility also play a factor in the economic impact outcomes.[17]

Notwithstanding these reservations, in contexts and communities where managers have no empirical data but are required by stakeholders to provide estimates of visitors' expenditures and economic impact, or need such estimates to help reposition their agency, the results from these case studies suggest useful parameters for providing "intelligent guesses".

The seven city park and recreation agencies that volunteered to participate in the study were: Boise, Idaho; College Station, Texas; Des Moines, Iowa; Everett, Washington; Grand Rapids, Michigan; Lansing, Michigan; and Scottsdale, Arizona. They were reasonably diverse in size and geographical location. Brief profiles of the seven cities are given in Table 10. The study was

Table 10 Profile of the Study Cities

Name	Location	Population Size	Median Income ($)
Boise	State capital and one of two metropolitan areas in Idaho	168,000	36,000
College Station	Brazos County, Texas, equidistant between Houston and Austin	66,000	29,000
Des Moines	The political, economic and cultural capital of Iowa, located in the heart of the state	200,000	42,000
Everett	The largest city in Snohomish County, Washington	80,000	46,000
Grand Rapids	West Michigan	192,000	44,000
Lansing	South-central lower Michigan, 90 miles west of Detroit	125,000	27,000
Scottsdale	In the Sonoran Desert at the base of the McDougall Mountains, Arizona	200,000	50,000

coordinated by the author and involved identifying the economic impact of 30 events held during a one year period in these seven cities. The author was responsible for designing the questionnaire; suggesting the sampling procedure; coding, entering and analyzing the data; and producing a written report for each of these events. The cities equally contributed to the cost of the study and provided personnel to collect the data.

Review of the Economic Impacts of 14 Sports Tournaments

A summary of results from the 14 team sports events that were studied is given in Table 11. To avoid the possibility of embarrassment to any of the cooperating cities, their identities have been protected and have been replaced by letter symbols which are shown in the left hand column. Columns 2 and 3 list the names of the events and their duration in days, respectively.

Sampling participants in team sports can be done either by surveying every n^{th} team or by surveying every n^{th} individual. In most cases, it is more convenient to sample teams since team members are often grouped together while waiting to play, practicing or at social gatherings. Column 4 shows that this was done in 11 of the 14 studies. In the remaining three studies, individuals were interviewed without reference to the teams they represented.

Column 5 reports the average size of the team squads. This information was obtained either from the questionnaire, or from event

Table 11 The Economic Impact of 14 Sports Tournaments

City	Event Name	Duration (# of Days)	# of Teams (# of Participants)	Average Size of Team Squad	# of Individual Participants	Teams from inside the city #	Teams from inside the city %	Teams from outside the city #	Teams from outside the city %	Total Expenditure	Average Direct Expenditures Per Team	Per Team Per Day	Per Team Member Group	Per Team Member Group Per Day	Economic Impact Sales	Personal Income	Jobs[a]
A	ASA Men's 40-Over Fastpitch National Championship	5	37	14	518	0	0.0	37	100.0	287,425	7,768	1,554	555	111	524,645	164,352	12.8
A	USS Swim Meet	3	24	45	1,079	2	8.3	22	91.7	124,999	5,682	1,894	126	42	236,852	64,201	5.3
A	Boys Soccer Tournament	3	68	15	1,020	5	7.4	63	92.6	128,519	2,040	680	136	45	247,085	69,493	5.7
A	Girls Soccer Tournament	3	70	15	1,050	0	0.0	70	100.0	160,956	2,299	766	153	51	305,070	85,889	6.8
A	Girls Fastpitch Invitational Tournament	3	69	12	828	15	21.7	54	78.3	184,517	3,417	1,139	285	95	351,588	99,811	8.0
B	Hoopin' Downtown Basketball Tournament	1	(584)	N/A	584	N/A	77.8	N/A	22.2	9,589	N/A	N/A	16	16	21,239	7,111	0.4
B	Great Plains Soccer Shoot Out Tournament	2	(1,800)	N/A	1,800	N/A	21.0	N/A	79.0	211,502	N/A	N/A	117	59	483,607	161,692	10.1
C	Magic Classic Softball Tournament	1	(900)	N/A	900	N/A	17.6	N/A	82.4	49,046	N/A	N/A	54	54	92,740	30,254	2.1
A	Whataburger Basketball Shoot Out	4	104	11	1,144	2	1.9	102	98.1	608,458	5,965	1,491	542	136	1,157,000	349,710	26.9
D	Girls U-14 Regional Softball Tournament	3	16	13	208	0	0.0	16	100.0	118,636	7,414	2,472	570	190	290,060	85,955	6.1
E	Invitational Youth Soccer Tournament	4	146	15	2,190	20	13.7	126	86.3	441,424	3,503	876	234	58	825,534	287,878	16.7
A	ASA Men's Fastpitch Softball Championship	3	28	14	392	1	3.6	27	96.4	93,219	3,453	1,151	247	82	176,903	50,904	4.0
A	ASA Men's B Fastpitch National Championship	5	60	14	840	2	3.3	58	96.7	386,999	6,672	1,334	477	95	730,973	211,870	16.7
E	Softball Tournaments	3 2 3	70 55 24	12	1,788	4 5 6	5.7 9.1 25.0	66 50 18	94.3 90.9 75.0	406,390	3,033	1,153	253	96	579,053	209,751	12.3

[a] This figure refers to both full-time and part-time jobs. It assumes the local economy is operating at full capacity and that there is no slack to absorb additional demand created by these events

organizers in those cases where teams were required to provide them with tournament rosters. Column 6 was derived by multiplying the data in columns 4 and 5.

It was noted in chapter 2 that economic impact referred only to the expenditures of visitors who resided outside the community. Columns 7 and 8 list the number and percentage of teams from within the city (or individuals in the three cases where teams were not surveyed). They were excluded from the analysis, which was confined only to those teams or individuals from outside the city. Their number and percentage is reported in columns 9 and 10.

The total expenditure shown in column 11 is derived by extrapolating the expenditures reported by the sample of external visitors to the total number of external visitors to the tournament. This calculation is illustrated and described in more detail in the sample report shown in Appendix 2. One of the dangers inherent in this procedure, especially if the sample is relatively small, is that a few extraordinary "outlier" responses in the sample can result in a large magnitude of error in the extrapolated results. Outliers are the very small number of respondents who report extraordinarily high (or low) expenditures, which would skew the study results because they are atypical. To rectify this potential error source, the author routinely disregarded the data collected from the 5% of respondents reporting the highest expenditures and the 5% reporting the lowest expenditures.

Columns 12 through 15, break down the total expenditure to a per team average (divide column 11 by column 9), per team per day (divide column 12 by column 3), per team member (divide column 11 by column 6), and per team member per day (divide column 14 by column 3). The purpose of these break downs is to establish common denominators across tournaments of different duration, with different numbers of teams and different sized squads. Standardizing the data in these ways facilitates the search for patterns and parameters in the data which is discussed in the next section of this chapter.

In chapter 2, it was noted that there were multiple measures of economic impact. The three which are most commonly cited are reported in columns 16 through 18. The measures were derived by entering the total expenditure data reported in column 11 into the IMPLAN model by category (there were 7 categories on the questionnaire shown in Figure 5).

Patterns and Parameters in the Sports Tournament Data

The data in Table 11 suggest the following:

1. The obvious and expected relationship that the larger the number of participants from *outside the community*, the greater the economic impact is likely to be.

2. If an overnight stay is not required, then the economic impact on the community is likely to be small. This exemplifies the retailing principle that the longer people remain in an area, the more they are likely to spend. Increasing visitors' average length of stay is the most efficient way to increase the economic impact of an event on the community. Hence, host agencies should vigorously promote attractions that may persuade participants to stay additional days in the local area. The highest total expenditures in column 11 correlate strongly with longer tournaments, which presumably required more overnight stays in the community. The two tournaments with the smallest economic impact were both one-day events. Such sports events appear unlikely to be sufficiently extensive or prestigious to attract visitors from far away and, hence, rely primarily on a

relatively local clientele. For example, two thirds of city B's Hoopin' Downtown Basketball Tournament participants, resided within the city, so the event's economic impact was minimal.

3.   Per team member group per day expenditures across the four boys and girls soccer tournaments were relatively consistent at $45, $51, $58 and $59, suggesting that an expectation of approximately $55 per day is likely to be a reasonable basis for estimating expenditures at youth soccer tournaments.

4.   Per team member group per day expenditures at the seven softball tournaments were $54, $82, $95, $95, $96, $111 and $190. The first and last numbers were extraordinary and unlikely to be typical. The first number relates to a tournament that lasted for only one day, so many participants were not required to stay overnight. The last number was caused by some of the teams travelling over 1,000 miles and, although the tournament was the trip's main purpose, the city's appealing location caused many to view the trip as a family vacation embracing other attractions in the area. This was reflected in the expenditures. The evidence of the other five studies suggests that an expenditure of approximately $100 per day is likely to be a reasonable basis for estimating expenditures at softball tournaments.

It is unclear why there is such a substantial difference in the expenditure of soccer and softball participants. Four possible explanations are commodification, climate, sub-culture and age cohorts. Conversations with sporting goods retailers suggests that softball players purchase personal equipment when they visit a community to play a tournament, but this is much less prevalent among soccer players. Such purchases may be stimulated by close interaction with other players for a multiple day period. The players are likely to have time blocks between tournament games when nothing is scheduled, and "hanging out" at stores that sell softball equipment is sometimes an appealing option. Soccer requires specialist clothing, but no personal equipment. Hence, the opportunities for commodification in the context of soccer are much fewer.

A second contributing factor to the differential economic impact of soccer and softball may be climate. If the climate during softball season is superior to that in the soccer season, then it may encourage participants to bring friends and families to a tournament and to engage in other activities. Third, there may be more of a gregarious "party", socialization sub-culture among softball than among soccer players which induces greater expenditures. Fourth, the four soccer tournaments that were surveyed were all youth events, while five of the seven softball tournaments were adult events. It seems intuitively reasonable that expenditures by adult participant groups would be substantially higher than those associated with youth groups.

It was noted in chapter 2 that the most useful measure of economic impact is increase in personal income, but that most tourist organizations report economic impact in terms of sales because it generates a much higher dollar number. This point is illustrated in Table 11 where the dollar impacts of sales shown in column 16 are typically between three and four times higher than the personal income measures listed in column 17.

Review of the Economic Impacts of 16 Festival and Spectator Events

The format of the analyses summary shown

in Table 12 is similar to that described in Table 11 with two exceptions. First, the columns relating to teams in Table 11 are not relevant to the analyses in Table 12 where the unit of analysis is individuals. Second, columns 8 and 9 relating to *time-switchers* and *casuals* did not appear in Table 11 because they were likely to be irrelevant in the context of sports tournaments. In chapter 2, *time-switchers* were defined as visitors to an event who have been planning a visit to the community for some time, but changed the timing of their visit to coincide with an event. The spending of these time-switchers should not be attributed to an event since it would have occurred without the event, albeit at a different time of the year. *Casuals* are visitors who are already in the community, attracted by other features, and who elected to go to the event instead of doing something else. Their spending in the community should not be attributed to the event, because if it had not been held, then their money would probably have been spent in the community on something else.

The total expenditures shown in column 12 are derived from two sources. First, visitors who were attracted to the community by the event. Second, the incremental amount spent by casuals and time-switchers which could be attributed to an extension of their stay in the community because of the event. More detail on how these were derived is given in the sample report included in Appendix 3.

Patterns and Parameters in the Festivals and Spectator Events Data.

The data in Table 12 suggest the following:

1.   Large numbers of participants and spectators do not necessarily equate to a large economic impact. For example, the Street Rod Run in city A and Golf Tour-

nament in city D, shown as the last two events in Table 12 attracted only 1409 and 1259 visitors, respectively. In contrast, the 4th of July Celebration in city F and Minor League Baseball games in city C attracted 55,000 and 16,895 visitors, respectively. However, the economic impacts of the Street Rod Run and Golf Tournament events were substantially greater than those accruing from the 4th of July Celebration or Minor League Baseball games (Columns 12 and 15). This is explained by the larger events lasting for only one day, and only 7% and 28% of the 4th of July Celebration and baseball games, respectively, visiting the communities specifically to participate in those events. Further, it seems likely that many out-of-town visitors commuted to these events from proximate communities, so their spending on accommodation and food in the host communities was likely to be small.

2.   The importance of ascertaining the proportion of visitors who are time-switchers and casuals is clearly demonstrated in columns 8 and 9. In five of the sixteen studies, time-switchers and casuals represented approximately one-third of all visitors. If the questionnaire had asked only for their home address or zip code and, therefore, failed to differentiate them from out-of-town visitors who were attracted specifically by the event, then there would have been a substantial over-estimation of the economic impact attributed to these events.

3.   Reasonably accurate measures of economic impact are dependent upon reasonably accurate counts of visitors to the events, because the impact estimates are derived by extrapolating from a sample to a total visitation count. In sports tournaments where teams or individuals have to register with the organizers, an accurate

Table 12 The Economic Impact of 16 Festival and Spectator Events

City	Event Name	Duration (# of Days)	Mean Length of Stay of Out-of-town Visitors	# of Visitor Days	Participants/Spectators from inside the city		Casuals/Time Switchers		Participants/Spectators from outside the city		Total[c] Expenditure	Average per Visitor per Day Expenditure	Economic Impact		
					#	%	#	%	#	%			Sales	Personal Income	Jobs[d]
G	Open Golf Tournament	3	2.4	464,000	140,167	30.2	72,500	15.6	251,333	54.2	29,523,070	117	65,856,795	22,389,187	1,232.0
G	Arts Festival	1	1.8	5,000	1,765	35.3	1,588	31.8	1,647	32.9	156,664	95	336,976	113,172	6.1
G	Culinary Festival	2	1.8	35,000	9,638	27.5	11,486	32.8	13,876	39.7	540,658	39	1,175,350	397,707	21.6
F	Annual Arts Festival	3	1.3	500,000	414,000	82.8	40,952	8.2	45,048	9.0	462,428	10	1,037,867	357,237	22.5
E	Rusty Relics Car Show	1	1.2	745[a]	46	6.2	0	0.0	699	93.8	6,562	9	12,500	3,894	0.3
C	Two Minor League Baseball Games	1 day each	1.0	16,895	6,735	39.9	5,438	32.2	4,722	27.9	25,225	5	54,184	17,818	1.3
C	Walk at the Zoo	1	1.1	525	153	29.2	195	37.1	177	33.7	548	3	1,055	345	0.0
C	Yes Festival	2	3.9	6,092	3,442	56.5	560	9.2	2,090	34.3	56,650	27	111,616	36,643	2.6
D	River Festival	4	3.1	1,000,000	135,135	13.5	369,574	37.0	495,291	49.5	5,781,136	12	14,698,137	4,442,505	326.0
F	4th of July Gala Celebration	1	1.7	55,000	48,605	88.4	2,398	4.3	3,997	7.3	34,420	9	74,793	25,474	1.5
E	Triathlon Dash	1	1.1	482[a]	94	19.5	38	7.9	350	72.6	14,841	42	25,693	11,416	0.5
F	Grand Prix Motor Race	3	1.6	85,000	72,425	85.2	4,899	5.8	7,676	9.0	172,764	23	382,446	129,902	7.8
E	Nubian Jam Heritage Celebration	1	1.7	5,000	2,041	40.8	877	17.5	2,082	41.7	32,356	16	64,715	19,678	1.4
D	Women's Fitness Challenge	1	1.3	105,415[a]	83,795	79.5	0	0.0	21,620	20.5	559,246	26	892,808	429,238	23.9
A	Bluebonnet Street Rod Run	3	2.2	1,409[a]	96	6.8	0	0.0	1,313	93.2	55,233	42	104,333	31,980	2.4
D	American Junior Golf Association Tournament	4	5.4	1,259[a]	0	0.0	0	0.0	1,259	100.0	74,868	59	188,414	56,690	4.0

a. The attendance data provided by the agencies for these events were in number of participants, and for purposes of consistency these were transformed in this table to number of visitor days, which includes members of participants' immediate groups.

b. This figure consists of the number of out-of-town visitors whose primary purpose of visit was to attend the event (Out-of-Towners), and the number of out-of-town visitors whose primary reason for their visit was not to attend the event but extended their stay because of it (Extended Stayers).

c. This figure consists of the expenditures by out-of-town visitors and extended stayers.

d. This figure refers to both full-time and part-time jobs. It assumes the local economy is operating at full capacity and that there is no slack to absorb additional demand created by these events.

count is usually available. Similarly, at gated spectator or festival events which charge an admission, accurate counts are available from ticket sales and/or turnstile counts. However, many festivals are not gated and do not charge admission. In these cases, attendance counts are frequently guesstimates made by the organizers. If these are inaccurate, then the economic impacts will be inaccurate. For example, if the River Festival attendance in Table 12 was actually 200,000 rather than 1 million[1], then the total expenditure would be $1.15 million rather than $5.78 million! Accuracy in sampling, data collection and analysis is of little use if the total attendance counts are inaccurate.

4.   Expenditures by out-of-town visitors exceeded $100,000 at 7 of the 16 special events (Table 12), whereas this figure was exceeded by 11 of the 14 sports tournaments (Table 11). These data suggest that a larger proportion of sports tournaments are likely to generate substantial positive economic impacts than special events, because of the higher proportion of participants who are from outside the community and the inherent requirement of many sports tournaments that participants stay in the community for multiple days. For small and medium sized communities that lack the resources to stage a large scale festival which will be sufficiently attractive that visitors will stay overnight, these data suggest that sports tournaments are likely to be a superior generator of positive economic impact.

5.   The extraordinary economic impact generated in a local community by a mega-event (as opposed to a typical community festival) is demonstrated by the first event listed in Table 12. This golf tournament was a stop on the men's professional tour. The very high total expenditure (column 12) not only reflects people staying multiple nights in the community and a large proportion of visitors from out-of-town, but also that the visitors are relatively affluent. The almost $30 million estimate in Table 12, is limited to the expenditures of spectators and does not include those by the players, officials and their entourages; the extensive number of media representatives; the hospitality expenditures of major companies, or sponsorships. Nevertheless, the $30 million expenditure dwarfs the aggregated $8 million and $3.3 million generated by the other 15 festivals and events shown in Table 12 and the 14 sports tournaments listed in Table 11, respectively.

6.   If an overnight stay is not required, then the economic impact on the community is likely to be relatively small. This reiterates the pattern noted in the sports tournament data. The per capita expenditure at single day events by out-of-town visitors were $95, $9, $5, $3, $9, $42, $16, and $26 (column 13). The three largest numbers had features that made them atypical one day events. At the Arts Festival, emphasis was on selling art rather than only viewing it. The $95 amount reflects this retailing dimension. Both the Triathlon Dash ($42) and the Women's Fitness Challenge ($26) had an overnight component, even though they were one day events. Many participants arrived in the community the previous evening so they would be rested before participating in the next day's athletic event.

---

[1]There is no reason to question the accuracy of this 1 million attendance estimate. It was arbitrarily selected to illustrate the point.

How to Present Economic Impact Results to Make the Economic Case

On several occasions in this publication it has been noted that although sales, personal income, and jobs are commonly reported measures of economic impact, the only meaningful measure for taxpayers and elected officials in local communities is the personal income that accrues to residents as a result of out-of-town visitor spending at the event. However, this creates an ethical conundrum for park and recreation managers since advocates from tourism, economic development, chambers of commerce, and other agencies, organizations and industrial sectors who seek to demonstrate their economic clout in a community are likely to use the relatively meaningless sales measure, because it is substantially bigger than the personal income measure, and the misleading employment measure.

If the economic impact of sports tournaments and special events is reported only by personal income, then it is likely to appear insignificant when compared to other economic sectors whose advocates report their impact in sales. The apparent relatively small impact of an event caused through reporting only the personal income measure may translate into commensurately less political and resource support for it from decision-makers and perhaps, ultimately, even withdrawal of appropriations for it. Acting ethically when others do not, could critically damage the event's standing. To resolve the conundrum, it is recommended that all three measures be reported so like measures can be compared to like, but that the limitations of the sales and jobs measures be emphasized. The following paragraphs offer a general template for this:

There is frequently confusion and misunderstanding in interpreting measures derived from the IMPLAN input-output model which are reported in columns 14, 15 and 16 of Table 12. It has become commonplace for tourism, economic development, and other agencies to report economic impact in terms of sales generated. In our view, this is of no value to elected officials or residents. It is used because it generates the highest economic impact number; but residents have no interest in sales generated, they are primarily interested in how it impacts them in terms of personal income.

The jobs' economic impact data often are similarly mischievously interpreted. For example, the arts festival in city G suggests that 6.1 jobs were created as a result of the festival. However, it seems reasonable to posit that local businesses are unlikely to hire additional full-time employees in response to additional demands created by the arts festival, because the extra business demand will last only for a few days. In these situations, the number of employees is not likely to increase. Rather, it is the number of hours that existing employees work that is likely to increase. Existing employees are likely to be requested to work overtime or to be released from other duties to accommodate this temporary peak demand. At best, only a few very short-term additional employees may be hired. Hence, it is improbable that anything like 6.1 jobs will be created.

This figure of 6.1 is further misleading because in calculating it, the model assumes (i) there was no spare capacity to absorb the extra services and products purchased with this inflow of new funds, and (ii) that no out-of-town residents took any new jobs that did emerge. In fact, the existing staff at hotels, restaurants, retail establishments, etc. are likely to have spare capacity to handle these visitors. If they do not, then it is likely that managers will reorganize shift schedules or pay overtime. Only if these adjustments are unable to accommodate the additional demand generated by the arts festival, will new jobs be created. Such jobs are likely to be temporary, part-time positions lasting for the duration of the festival.

The most useful economic impact indicator is that which measures the event's contribution to the personal incomes of residents. This is rarely used by tourism agencies because it is generally three to four times smaller than the sales impact. However, it is the indicator that is likely to be most meaningful to residents.

Agencies should prepare an annual economic impact report each year for their stakeholders. Extrapolations can be made from data included in this report to similar events in the community that were not surveyed. An example taken from sports tournaments in city A, is shown in Table 13. Data from the six sports events listed above the bold line in Table 13 were collected by surveys. No surveys were undertaken at the four events below the line. These events were matched with above-the-line events that were most similar and the per team member per day dollar value was used from the matching events to calculate the total expenditure and economic impacts.

The economic impact report in Table 13 shows that almost $1 million accrued in new income to city residents, and that out-of-town visitor expenditures resulted in over $3 million of additional sales. This balance sheet

was presented to city A's council as part of the budget process and helped solidify the department's position as a contributor to economic development.

Similarly, an annual balance sheet showing the economic impact of special events sponsored by city F is shown in Table 14. It was derived by extrapolating results from 3 special events in this city that were surveyed to an additional 10 events which were sponsored by the city during the year but at which no data were collected. The ratios of visitors from inside the city, casuals/time switchers, and visitors from outside the city were similar at all of the 3 surveyed events. This suggested that it was reasonable to extrapolate to the other events, the average ratios of the 3 surveyed events of 85.5, 6.1 and 8.4 for the local residents, casuals/time switchers, and out-of-town visitors, respectively.

Attendance estimates for the 10 non-surveyed events were available. The per capita spending by out-of-town visitors at the three surveyed events was $10.26 (462,428 ÷ 45,048), $8.61, and $22.50, yielding an average of $13.79. This number was used to calculate the total expenditure at the non-surveyed events. For example, the $18,623 total expenditure at Winter Fest was derived by $13.79 x 1350.

Arraying the economic return from special events in this way also offers managers and stakeholders guidelines as to which should receive priority in promotional effort. The spending of visitors to the Grand Prix was $22.50 per visitor, compared to $10.25 and $8.61 for the Arts Festival and Gala Celebration, respectively. This suggests that the most efficient strategy for city F to increase its return on investment may be to focus on out-of-town visitors to the Grand Prix, rather than on the other two events.

There are many legitimate reasons for sponsoring festivals and special events beyond their contribution to economic devel-

Table 13   The Economic Impact of Team Sports Events Held in City A

Event Name	Date	Duration (# of Days)	# of Teams	Average Size of Team Squad	# of Individual Participants	Teams from inside the city #	Teams from inside the city %	Teams from outside the city #	Teams from outside the city %	Total Expenditure	Average Direct Expenditures Per Team	Per Team Per Day	Per Team Member	Per Team Member Per Day	Sales	Personal Income	Jobs[a]
USS Swim Meet	1-23	3	24	45	1,079	2	8.3	22	91.7	124,999	5,682	1,894	126	42	236,852	64,201	5.3
Boys Soccer Tournament	2-20	3	68	15	1,020	5	7.4	63	92.6	128,519	2,040	680	136	45	247,085	69,493	5.7
Girls Soccer Tournament	2-28	3	70	15	1,050	0	0.0	70	100.0	160,956	2,299	766	153	51	305,070	85,889	6.8
Girls Fastpitch Invitational Tournament	5-29	3	69	12	828	15	21.7	54	78.3	184,517	3,417	1,139	285	95	351,588	99,811	8.0
ASA Men's Fastpitch Softball Championship	8-1	3	28	14	392	1	3.7	27	96.4	93,219	3,453	1,151	247	82	176,903	50,904	4.0
ASA Men's Class B National Championship	9-7	5	60	14	840	2	3.3	58	96.7	386,999	6,672	1,334	477	95	730,973	211,870	16.7
Budweiser Tournament	5-2	2	162	14	2,268	30	18.5	132	81.5	303,864	2,302	1,151	164	82	440,655	151,729	9.8
State Girls Fastpitch U-18	7-10	3	34	12	408	1	2.9	33	97.1	112,761	3,417	1,139	285	95	163,523	56,305	3.6
Men's Slowpitch State Class C	7-24	3	101	14	1,414	14	13.9	87	86.1	300,411	3,453	1,151	247	82	435,648	150,005	9.6
State Women's Fastpitch	8-1	2	5	12	60	0	0.0	5	100.0	11,390	2,278	1,139	190	95	16,517	5,687	0.4
Total	-	-	621	-	9,359	70	11.3	551	88.7	1,807,635	-	-	-	-	3,104,814	945,894	69.9

a.   This figure refers to both full-time and part-time jobs. It assumes the local economy is operating at full capacity and that there is no slack to absorb additional demand created by these events.

Table 14 The Economic Impact of Special Events Held in City F

Event Name	Date	Duration (# of Days)	# of Visitor Days	Participants/ Spectators from inside the city #	%	Casuals/Time Switchers #	%	Participants/[a] Spectators from outside the city #	%	Total[b] Expenditure	Economic Impact Sales	Personal Income	Jobs[c]
Annual Arts Festival	6-5	3	500,000	414,000	82.8	40,952	8.2	45,048	9.0	462,428	1,037,867	357,237	22.5
4th of July Gala Celebration	7-4	1	55,000	48,605	88.4	2,398	4.3	3,997	7.3	34,420	74,793	25,474	1.5
Grand Prix Motor Race	7-24	3	85,000	72,425	85.2	4,899	5.8	7,676	9.0	172,764	382,446	129,902	7.8
WinterFest	1-23	2	16,000	13,674	85.5	976	6.1	1,350	8.4	18,623	28,724	11,025	0.6
Three Fires Pow Wow	6-13	2	25,000	21,365	85.5	1,525	6.1	2,110	8.4	29,107	44,894	17,231	0.9
African-American Festival	7-10	3	15,000	12,819	85.5	915	6.1	1,266	8.4	17,464	26,936	10,339	0.5
Jazz & Blues Festival	7-31	2	10,000	8,546	85.5	610	6.1	844	8.4	11,643	17,958	6,893	0.4
Italian Festival	8-7	3	30,000	25,638	85.5	1,830	6.1	2,532	8.4	34,929	53,874	20,678	1.1
Polish Harvest Festival	8-28	3	15,000	12,819	85.5	915	6.1	1,266	8.4	17,464	26,936	10,339	0.5
German Festival	9-4	3	10,000	8,546	85.5	610	6.1	844	8.4	11,643	17,958	6,893	0.4
Celebration on the Grand	9-11	2	350,000	299,110	85.5	21,350	6.1	29,540	8.4	407,504	628,529	241,239	12.7
Hispanic Festival	9-11	3	70,000	59,822	85.5	4,270	6.1	5,908	8.4	81,501	125,706	48,248	2.5
Mexican Festival	9-18	3	100,000	85,460	85.5	6,100	6.1	8,440	8.4	116,430	179,580	68,926	3.6
Total	-	-	1,281,000	1,082,829		87,350		110,821		1,415,920	2,646,201	954,424	55.0

a. This figure consists of the number of out-of-town visitors whose primary purpose of visit was to attend the event (Out-of-Towners), and the number of out-of-town visitors whose primary reason for their visit was not to attend the event but extended their stay because of it (Extended Stayers).

b. This figure consists of the expenditures by out-of-town visitors and extended stayers.

c. This figure refers to both full-time and part-time jobs. It assumes the local economy is operating at full capacity and that there is no slack to absorb additional demand created by these events.

opment. However, *if* economic development is the prime consideration, then these analyses offer a basis for prioritizing which events are most viable. When the agency's cost of organizing an event is considered along with the community infrastructure, displacement and opportunity costs discussed in chapter 2, the relatively small impact on personal income suggests that the viability of some of the sponsored events shown in Table 14 may be challengeable.

Finally, in reports to stakeholders it is worth noting that in addition to the economic impact attributable to the specific events which is reported, events may stimulate subsequent tourism. Initial exposure to the community may cause some visitors to return in the future as tourists, or to encourage their friends to visit the community.

THE THREE COLLECTIVE "PUBLIC" BENEFITS THAT MAY ACCRUE FROM PARK AND RECREATION SERVICES[1]

The provision of park and recreation opportunities for their own sake still lacks political clout. They have to be shown to solve community problems before politicians see them as being worthy of funding. Many taxpayers are not frequent users of park and recreation services and, thus, have difficulty understanding why they should support them. The prevailing sentiment is often: If only some segments of our community use park and recreation services, then why should the rest of us have to pay for them? To gain the support of non-users, an agency has to provide a convincing answer to the question "What is in it for them?" Broader community support is likely to be dependent on building awareness not only of the on-site benefits that accrue to users, but also of the off-site benefits that accrue to non-users in communities.

There is increased recognition that while benefit driven programs may lead to higher levels of satisfaction among participants and attract increased numbers, such individual "private" benefits have relatively little impact on resource allocation decisions made by elected officials. These benefits are described as individual or "private" because they accrue only to program participants and do not extend to the majority of the population who are only occasional users or non-users. Providing resources to a parks and recreation department so a minority of residents can have enjoyable experiences is likely to be a low priority when measured against the critical economic, health, safety and welfare issues with which most legislative bodies are confronted.

To justify the allocation of additional resources, elected officials have to be convinced that park and recreation agencies deliver collective "public" benefits. These are defined as benefits that accrue to most people in a community, even though they do not participate in an agency's programs or use its facilities. There are just three of these public benefits: **economic development; alleviat-**

---

[1]   An expanded discussion of these benefits can be found in Chapter 5 of a book: John L. Crompton (1999) *Financing and Acquiring Park and Recreation Resources*, Champaign, Illinois: Human Kinetics.

ing social problems; and environmental stewardship. However, even these three categories of public benefits receive funding support only when they are regarded as being high priority in a community. Hence, the task of a park and recreation agency is to identify which of these public benefits is most prominent on a jurisdiction's political agenda, and to demonstrate the agency's potential contribution to fulfilling that agenda.

Economic Development

Economic development is viewed as a means of enlarging the tax base. The enlargement provides more tax revenues that governments can use either to improve the community's infrastructure, facilities, and services or to reduce the level of taxes that existing residents pay. It is seen also as a source of jobs and income that enables residents to improve their quality of life. In some communities, park and recreation agencies play a major role in economic development. That role may take the form of:

(i) **Attracting Tourists**: The major factor considered by tourists when they make a decision which communities to visit on a pleasure trip, is the attractions that are available. In most cities, those attractions are dominated by facilities and services operated by park and recreation agencies and their nonprofit partners (parks, beaches, events, festivals, athletic tournaments, museums, historical sites, cultural performances, etc.). Without such attractions, there is no tourism.

(ii) **Attracting Businesses**: The viability of businesses in the highly recruited high-technology, research and development, company headquarters, and services sectors, in many cases is dependent on their ability to attract and retain highly educated profes-

sional employees. The deciding factor of where these individual choose to live is often the quality of life in the geographic vicinity of the business. No matter how quality of life is defined, park and recreation opportunities are likely to be a major component of it.

(iii) **Attracting Retirees**. A new clean growth industry in America today is the growing number of relatively affluent, active retirees. Their decisions as to where to locate with their substantial retirement incomes is primarily governed by two factors: climate and recreational opportunities.

(iv) **Enhancing Real Estate Values**. People are prepared to pay more to live close to natural park areas. The enhanced value of these properties results in their owners paying higher property taxes to governments. If the incremental amount of taxes paid by each property that is attributable to the park is aggregated, it is often sufficient to pay the annual debt charges required to retire the bonds used to acquire and develop the park.

Alleviating Social Problems

(i) **Preventing Youth Crime**. The use of park and recreation programs to alleviate youth crime was a primary political stimulant for much of the early recreation provision in major cities at the beginning of the 20th century. There is strong evidence demonstrating the success of these programs when they are structured to provide: social support from adult leaders; leadership opportunities for youth; intensive and individualized attention to participants; a sense of group belonging; youth input into program decisions; and opportunities for community service. The return on investment of such programs is substantial when it is related to the costs of incarceration.

(ii) **Healthy Lifestyles**. There is growing recognition that the key to curtailing health care costs lies in prevention of illness so it does not have to be treated by the expensive medical system. Park and recreation services contribute to this end not only by facilitating improvements in physical fitness through exercise, but also by facilitating positive emotional, intellectual and social experiences. People with high levels of wellness have a proclivity to act during their free time, rather than merely be acted on.

(iii) **Environmental Stress**. Environmental stress may involve both psychological emotions, such as frustrations, anger, fear and coping responses, and associated physiological responses that use energy and contribute to fatigue. It is experienced daily by many who live or commute in urban or blighted areas. Parks in urban settings have a restorative effect that releases the tensions of modern life. Evidence demonstrating the therapeutic value of natural settings has emerged in both physiological and psychological studies. The cost of environmental stress in terms of work days lost and medical care is likely to be substantially greater than the cost of providing and maintaining parks, urban forestry programs, and oases of flowers and shrubs.

(iv) **Unemployment and Underemployment**. Basic psychological needs that many people derive from their work are difficult to acquire when unemployed or working in low-level service jobs such as cashiers, janitors and cleaners which are the major growth positions in the economy. Such needs may include self-esteem, prestige accruing from peer group recognition, ego satisfaction of achievement, a desire to be successful, excitement and self-worth. For the growing number of people in low level jobs, these needs will be obtained in their familial or leisure milieus, or they will not be obtained at all.

Environmental Stewardship

(i) **Historical Preservation**. Without a cultural history, people are rootless. Preserving historical remnants offers lingering evidence to remind people of what they once were, who they are, what they are and where they are. It feeds their sense of history.

(ii) **The Natural Environment**. People turn to the natural environment, preserved by humans as a park, wilderness, or wildlife refuge, for something they cannot get in a built environment. The quality of human life depends on an ecological sustainable and aesthetically pleasing physical environment. The surge of interest in conserving open spaces from people motivated by ecological and aesthetic concerns, is matched by a similar surge from those concerned that the inexorable rise in demands for outdoor recreation is not being matched by a commensurate expansion of the supply base.

GUIDELINES FOR SURVEYORS[1]

Thank you for agreeing to serve on the survey team. We appreciate your valuable contribution to this very important project. The following information will help you understand the project and what you will need to do.

1. **Purpose**: The purpose of the survey is to determine, by scientific sampling methods, the economic value of Springfest to Ocean City. Selected visitors to Springfest are being asked to complete a survey form which will provide enough information for us to be able to calculate the dollar impact on the community of all visitor spending during the festival.

2. **Survey Development**: The survey instrument was developed by Dr. John Crompton of Texas A&M University and modified by the staff of the Town of Ocean City so it related specifically to Springfest.

3. **Survey Composition**: The survey instrument consists of 6 questions all of which are contained on one side of a piece of paper. All the questions are important. The survey is only one page so respondents can complete it in a relatively short period of time and be on their way. (*A copy of the survey is given in chapter 3*).

4. **Survey Completion Time**: The survey is likely to take approximately 90 seconds to complete. This time estimate should be provided when approaching potential survey respondents. Some respondents may take more than 90 seconds because some of the questions involve estimating amounts of money to be spent. This section of the survey is likely to be the most difficult part to complete for most people.

5. **Survey Audience**: The target audience for this survey is people who are visiting Springfest from *outside* the local area. Since there is no way of distinguishing visitors from outside the area in a crowd from "locals", a definition is used to separate them.

[1] These guidelines were developed by Tom Shuster, Recreation and Parks Director for the Town of Ocean City, Maryland for use at a 1 hour pre-event training program undertaken with surveyors who were collecting economic impact data at the Springfest Festival. Space is left between the questions to enable those being trained to make notes.

6. **Locals**: For the purposes of this survey only, locals are defined as people who have their *primary* residence in Ocean City (zip codes 21842 or 21843), Berlin (21811), or Bishopville (21813). Individuals with one of these 4 zip codes are considered to be part of the Ocean City economy and are classified as "locals". Since people already living in the local economy aren't bringing in any new money from the outside, they are not a part of the target audience for this survey.

7. **Surveys Needed**: For the economic results to be reasonably accurate, a total of 800 surveys will need to be taken from visitors attending from outside the area over the 4 days of Springfest. This equates to approximately 200 surveys taken per day. The number may vary by day. However, 800 total surveys are needed.

8. **Survey Teams**: Survey takers will be grouped into teams of 2 people. Teams will work a defined area on the festival grounds near one of the 2 primary entrances. There is no admission charge to Springfest. There are multiple entrances to the site but two of them account for a large proportion of visitors. Teams will be assigned specific hours to work during the festival. Hours of work may vary from day to day.

9. **Support To Survey Teams**: Support to the survey teams will be provided by staff of the Special Events Division and other Town employees working at Springfest.

10. **Identification**: As a survey taker you will be an official representative of the Town of Ocean City. You will be provided with appropriate apparel to identify you as a part of Springfest.

11. **Preparedness**: Come to work each day prepared for your assignment and your time

shift. Dress comfortably and wear comfortable shoes. Bring along other protective clothing if there is the possibility of inclement weather.

Be prepared to approach strangers. Put on your best smile and your most assertive attitude. Before your first day actually imagine yourself approaching people. Try to see yourself performing the entire sequence of steps from approaching through completing the survey process.

12. **Selecting Someone to Approach**: For this survey to be scientific it must be as random as possible. To facilitate randomness, a uniform method is used to determine who to approach to complete a survey.

Each survey taker is asked to count the flow of people approaching him/her. The survey taker remains in one place as people pass by. When the survey taker counts the 8th person, then that person is the target person.

However, approach only adult males or females to complete the survey. So, for example, if the 8th person you count is a child or youth, then don't approach him/her, but if an adult is part of the group, then the adult should be approached. If the group does not include any adults, then skip to the next adult after them.

The counting may have to be approximate, rather than exact, at times when the flow of the crowd is heavy or fast. Remember the purpose of the counting is to create a reasonably random, uniform interval.

13. **Your Opening Approach**: When approaching someone to interview, move toward them and make eye contact. Smile and greet them with the following opening. "Hi, I'm on the Springfest Staff." At this point

pause to make sure you have made eye contact. "Could you please take a moment to help us by completing this important survey." Hold up a clip board with the survey. "It will only take about 90 seconds to complete and will help us to improve Springfest."

If they agree, or if they hesitate, ask them "What's your zip code" which is the first question.

If they answer the zip code question and it is not one of the local codes (21842, 21843, 21811 or 21813), immediately hand them the clip board and ask them to complete the survey and return it to you.

If they answer the zip code question by saying it is one of the local codes (21842, 21843, 21811 or 21813), say "Thanks, you've just completed the survey. Wasn't that easy." You must now record the local "hit" on a separate counting sheet. After recording the local zip, start your random 8 count again.

If the person you approach doesn't answer the zip code question and continues walking, let him/her go. Resume your random 8 count and start a new approach.

Survey experience shows that up to 15% of people approached to participate in a survey in this manner refuse to respond. Some people just don't want to be bothered by surveys or may have other reasons for refusing. Don't take the lack of a positive response as a personal rejection.

Their decision has little to do with you. Simply go on to your next prospective survey respondent.

14. **Self-Administered Survey**: After you have selected and approached the chosen respondent, and he/she has agreed to participate, he/she completes the survey. Hand the individual the clip board which has the survey on it and a pen attached as well.

Ask selected individuals to step behind you out of the way of the crowd to complete the survey. Ask them to return the survey to you when it is completed. Remember it should take them about 90 seconds to complete. Put their survey in the completed survey box when they return it to you.

15. **Monitoring**: Your survey work will be monitored by the Springfest staff to help ensure consistency. If you have any questions be sure to ask them.

TEMPLATE FOR A REPORT OF THE ECONOMIC IMPACT OF A SPORTS TOURNAMENT

The ASA Men's 40 and Over Fast pitch National Softball Championship Tournament was held in city A in August 1998. A total of 28 teams participated in the tournament. Since economic impact is concerned only with new money coming into the community, the analyses reported here focus on the 27 teams which came from outside the local area.

Data from which the conclusions in this study are based were collected from 84 players, who were associated with 23 of the 27 teams. On seven of these teams only 1 or 2 respondents were surveyed, so their responses were combined into one "team" in the analysis which was named, "Other". The average number of players on each team was 14, but squads ranged in size from 11 to 18 players (Table 1).

The economic impact was calculated by using a four stage process. First, the sample of respondents from the 17 teams were asked how much they spent in the city A area. Their expenditures were assigned to eight categories: food and beverages; entrance fees (these were derived directly from the host agency); entertainment, bars and night clubs; retail shopping; lodging; private auto; rental car; and other. The questionnaire used to collect the data is included at the back of this report. (*It is shown as Figure 5 in chapter 3 of this publication*) The data collected from respondents in this first stage showing the average per-group expenditures are shown in Table 2.

Stage two was to extrapolate the data collected from the samples of respondents from these 17 teams, so that it represented the expenditures of all members of their teams. This was done in Table 3, which shows the extrapolated total expenditures associated with each team in each of the seven spending categories. Thus in Table 2, the average expenditure reported by each respondent on the Aledo Team for food and beverages was $85. The respondents were unsure about how many players were on their squad. Some reported 12 and others 13, but the average was 12.25. Hence, the team expenditures on food and beverages were estimated at $1,041 ($85 × 12.25) in Table 3.

Stage three was to extrapolate the average expenditures of the 17 teams shown in the last row of Table 3 to the full complement of

27 teams from outside the local area which participated in the tournament. Table 4 shows that **total expenditures from all 17 teams were approximately $93,219**.

The final stage was to estimate the impact of this new money on the local economy. This was done by using the IMPLAN input-output model for the city. It shows that **total impact on sales was $176,903** (Table 5), **impact on personal income was $50,904** (Table 6), and **the job creation impact was estimated at 4.04 jobs** (Table 7).

There is frequently confusion and misunderstanding in interpreting these multipliers. It has become commonplace for tourism economic development and other agencies to report economic impact in terms of sales generated. In our view, this is of no value to elected officials or residents. It is used because it generates the highest economic impact number; but residents have no interest in sales generated, they are primarily interested in how it personally impacts them in terms of personal income.

The jobs' economic impact data often are similarly mischievously interpreted. Table 7 suggests that 4.04 jobs were created as a result of the tournament. However, it seems reasonable to posit that local businesses are unlikely to hire additional full-time employees in response to additional demands created by the tournament, because the extra business demand will last only for a few days. In these situations, the number of employees is not likely to increase. Rather, it is the number of hours that existing employees work that is likely to increase. Existing employees are likely to be requested to work overtime or to be released from other duties to accommodate this temporary peak demand. At best, only a few very short-term additional employees may be hired. Hence, it is improbable that anything like 4.04 jobs will be created.

This figure of 4.04 is further misleading because in calculating it, the model assumes (i) there was no spare capacity to absorb the extra services and products purchased with this inflow of new funds, and (ii) that no out-of-town residents took any new jobs that did emerge. In fact, the existing staff at hotels, restaurants, retail establishments, etc. are likely to have spare capacity to handle these visitors. If they do not, then it is likely that managers will reorganize shift schedules or pay overtime. Only if these adjustments are unable to accommodate the additional demand generated by the tournament, will new jobs be created. Such jobs are likely to be temporary, part-time positions lasting for the duration of the tournament.

The most useful economic impact indicator is that which measures the tournament's contribution to the personal incomes of residents in city A, which amounted to $50,904 (Table 6). This is rarely used by tourism agencies because it is so small compared to the sales impact. In this case, it is more than three times smaller than the sales impact. However, it is the indicator that is likely to be most meaningful to residents.

Table 1	Number of Players on Teams that were Surveyed	
Number of Players	Number of Teams	Percentage
11	1	6%
12	5	29%
13	1	6%
14	5	29%
15	3	18%
16	1	6%
18	1	6%

Table 2 Data from Respondent Surveys showing Average Per-Respondent Group Expenditures ($)

Team Name	City	# of Players	Food & Beverages	Night Clubs, Lounge, Bar	Retail Shopping	Lodging Expenses	Private Auto Expenses	Rental Car	Other Expenses
Aledo	Aledo	12	85	0	6	105	21	6	1
Amarillo A's	Amarillo	12	55	5	25	73	13	0	5
Austin Roadrunners	Austin	12	52	17	4	120	22	0	3
Aztecs	Port Arthur	14	138	13	34	63	26	0	0
Beaumont/Port Arthur Miller Lite	Beaumont/Port Arthur	14	76	19	39	84	30	0	3
Caldwell Team	Caldwell	12	70	25	100	0	48	0	0
Castro Concrete Jokers	Austin	14	20	0	0	105	10	0	0
F&F Strikers	Beaumont	14	125	13	32	112	35	0	25
Houston 9	Houston	11	70	11	19	50	9	0	0
Manor Rangers	Manor	14	104	6	59	130	31	0	5
Sharks	Galveston	13	103	0	33	70	17	0	0
Texas 7	Brenham	16	80	0	58	48	43	0	0
Texas Flyers	Houston	15	77	0	40	58	32	0	0
Velvet Elvis	Dallas	15	113	0	4	160	20	0	0
War Bucks	Livingston	15	36	10	82	42	27	0	0
Yoakum Fast Pitch	Yoakum	18	138	14	38	109	38	0	0
Other	-	12	109	43	34	113	31	11	1
Average		13	91	14	36	89	28	2	3

Table 3 Expenditures by Each of the Sampled Teams ($)

Team Name	Food & Beverages	Night Clubs, Lounge, Bar	Retail Shopping	Lodging Expenses	Private Auto Expenses	Rental Car	Other Expenses	Total
Aledo	1,041	0	77	1,286	256	77	12	2,749
Amarillo A's	646	59	294	852	147	0	59	2,056
Austin Roadrunners	628	200	48	1,440	260	0	40	2,616
Aztecs	1,925	175	473	875	368	0	0	3,815
Beaumont/Port Arthur Miller Lite	1,092	265	551	1,204	429	0	41	3,643
Caldwell Team	799	288	1,150	0	546	0	0	2,783
Castro Concrete Jokers	280	0	0	1,470	140	0	0	1,890
F&F Strikers	1,771	189	449	1,584	496	0	354	4,925
Houston 9	788	127	211	563	98	0	0	1,786
Manor Rangers	1,477	85	835	1,846	440	0	68	5,121
Sharks	1,378	0	444	933	222	0	0	2,978
Texas 7	1,280	0	933	773	693	0	0	3,680
Texas Flyers	1,124	0	587	846	464	0	0	3,021
Velvet Elvis	1,716	0	57	2,440	305	0	0	4,518
War Bucks	547	152	1,246	638	410	0	0	2,994
Yoakum Fast Pitch	2,421	248	656	1,913	656	0	0	5,895
Other	1,325	521	410	1,379	383	133	17	4,223
Average	1,190	136	495	1,179	371	12	35	3,453

Table 4 Total Expenditures by the 27 Out-of-Town Teams in the City A Area

Items	Expenditures ($)
Food and Beverages	32,143
Entrance Fees	903
Night Clubs, Lounges, and Bars	3,666
Retail Shopping	13,375
Lodging Expenses	31,833
Private Auto Expenses	10,028
Commercial Transportation	333
Other Expenses	938
Total	93,219

Table 5 Economic Impact on Sales

Items	Sales Coefficient				Economic Impact ($)
	Direct	Indirect	Induced	Total	
Food and Beverages	1	0.2396	0.6678	1.9074	61,309
Entrance Fees	1	0.0000	0.6647	1.6647	1,503
Night Clubs, Lounges, Bars	1	0.2396	0.6678	1.9074	6,993
Retail Shopping	1	0.2007	0.9761	2.1768	29,114
Lodging Expenses	1	0.3337	0.5385	1.8722	59,597
Private Auto Expenses	1	0.2222	0.3339	1.5561	15,604
Commercial Transportation	1	0.3222	0.3286	1.6508	550
Other Expenses	1	0.3320	1.0480	2.3800	2,233
Total					176,903

Table 6 Economic Impact on Personal Income

Items	Personal Income Coefficient				Economic Impact ($)
	Direct	Indirect	Induced	Total	
Food and Beverages	0.3114	0.0572	0.1859	0.5545	17,823
Entrance Fees	0.9071	0.0000	0.1850	1.0921	986
Night Clubs, Lounges, Bars	0.3114	0.0572	0.1859	0.5545	2,033
Retail Shopping	0.3175	0.0471	0.2717	0.6362	8,509
Lodging Expenses	0.2816	0.0840	0.1499	0.5154	16,407
Private Auto Expenses	0.2953	0.0539	0.0929	0.4421	4,433
Commercial Transportation	0.2140	0.0815	0.0914	0.3869	129
Other Expenses	0.2500	0.0817	0.2917	0.6233	585
Total					50,904

Table 7 Economic Impact on Employment

Items	Employment Coefficient				Impact on Employment (people) *
	Direct	Indirect	Induced	Total	
Food and Beverages	31.1281	3.1226	11.5072	45.7579	1.47
Entrance Fees	34.0891	0.0000	11.4529	45.5420	0.04
Night Clubs, Lounges, Bars	31.1281	3.1226	11.5072	45.7579	0.17
Retail Shopping	46.7848	2.6580	16.8191	66.2619	0.89
Lodging Expenses	22.4055	5.2113	9.2784	36.8952	1.17
Private Auto Expenses	14.0035	3.1202	5.7530	22.8768	0.23
Commercial Transportation	11.7274	5.1242	5.6616	22.5132	0.01
Other Expenses	48.2091	4.8750	18.0578	71.1419	0.07
Total					4.04

* This figure refers to both full-time and part-time jobs. It assumes the local economy is operating at full capacity and that there is no slack to absorb additional demand created by these events

TEMPLATE FOR A REPORT OF THE ECONOMIC IMPACT OF A SPECIAL EVENT

Minor League Baseball Games were held in city C on June 17 and 23, 1998. The games attracted 16,895 visitors. Interviews were conducted with 434 visitors attending the games. 60% of respondents came from outside city C (Table 1), but over half of these visitors would have come to city C if the game had not been held (Table 2). Among those from outside the city who would have visited the area without the event taking place, only 5% extended their stay in the community because of the event (Table 3). In subsequent analyses, these respondents were termed "Extended Stayers".

Because economic impact is concerned only with new money entering into the city from outside its boundaries, the analyses disregarded respondent groups who were local residents, and those visitor groups who came from outside the city's boundaries but who would have come to the city C area even if the games had not been held and did not extend their stay because of it. Thus, subsequent analyses were confined to the 26% of visitors who were Out-of-Towners and who would not have come to city C if the games had not been held, and the 2% of visitors classified as Extended Stayers. The economic impact of these two groups could be attributed to the baseball games.

The unit of analysis for collecting the data and estimating economic impact was the immediate group, which was defined as the set of individuals for whom one person paid the expenses. The mean group sizes for the Out-of-Towners and Extended Stayers were 5.09 and 3.67, respectively (Table 4). The questionnaire, which is included at the back of the report, captured information on respondents' expenditures associated with visiting the game. (*The questionnaire is shown as Figure 5 in chapter 3 of this publication*) This enabled a calculation to be made of the per group, per day expenditures.

In situations such as this where very small samples are used to extrapolate to large populations, a few extraordinary "outlier" responses in the sample, can result in a very large magnitude of error in the extrapolated results. To rectify this problem, responses were disregarded from those giving the 5% highest and lowest spending estimates. The results after taking these actions are reported in Table 5.

Table 5 shows the average per group per day expenditures. These were extrapolated to the proportion of game visitors who were Out-of-Towners (4,427) and Extended Stayers (295) in Table 6. Thus, food and beverages for the city C area totaled (19.79 (Table 5) x 4,427 ÷ 5.09) + (5.85 (Table 5) x 295 ÷ 3.67), which yielded the $17,685 ($17,215 + $470) shown in Table 6. These results show that **the estimate of economic impact as measured by direct expenditures was $28,251** ($25,222 from Out-of-Towners and $3,029 from Extended Stayers).

The next stage was to estimate the impact of this new money on the city C economy. This was done by using the IMPLAN input-output model for the city. Tables 7 and 8 show **the estimated economic impact measured after sales multipliers were applied was $54,184** ($48,260 + $5,924). A more useful measure of economic impact is its effect on the income of city residents. Tables 9 and 10 show **the estimated economic impact on personal income was estimated at $17,818**. Finally, Tables 11 and 12 **estimate that the games created 1.27 jobs**.

There is frequently confusion and misunderstanding in interpreting these multipliers. It has become commonplace for tourism, economic development, and other agencies to report economic impact in terms of sales generated. In our view, this is of no value to elected officials or residents. It is used because it generates the highest economic impact number; but residents have no interest in sales generated, they are primarily interested in how it personally impacts them in terms of personal income.

The jobs' economic impact data often are similarly mischievously interpreted. Tables 11 and 12 suggest that 1.27 jobs were created as a result of the games. However, it seems reasonable to posit that local businesses are unlikely to hire additional full-time employ-

ees in response to additional demands created by the game, because the extra business demand will last only for a few days. In these situations, the number of employees is not likely to increase. Rather, it is the number of hours that existing employees work that is likely to increase. Existing employees are likely to be requested to work overtime or to be released from other duties to accommodate this temporary peak demand. At best, only a few very short-term additional employees may be hired. Hence, it is improbable that anything like 1.27 jobs will be created.

This figure of 1.27 is further misleading because in calculating it, the model assumes (i) there was no spare capacity to absorb the extra services and products purchased with this inflow of new funds, and (ii) that no out-of-town residents took any new jobs that did emerge. In fact, the existing staff at hotels, restaurants, retail establishments, etc. are likely to have spare capacity to handle these visitors. If they do not, then it is likely that managers will reorganize shift schedules or pay overtime. Only if these adjustments are unable to accommodate the additional demand generated by the game, will new jobs be created. Such jobs are likely to be temporary, part-time positions lasting for the duration of the game.

The most useful economic impact indicator is that which measures the contribution of the baseball games to the personal incomes of residents in city C, which amounted to $17,818 (Tables 9 and 10). This is rarely used by tourism agencies because it is so small compared to the sales impact. In this case, it is three times smaller than the sales impact. However, it is the indicator that is likely to be most meaningful to residents.

Table 1	Visitor Group Origin	
Origin	Number of Groups	Percentage
Out-of-Town	261	60%
City C Residents	173	40%

Table 2 Out-of-Town Visitor Groups who would have visited city C even in the game had not been held

	Number of Groups	Percentage
Yes	136	56%
No	105	44%

Table 3 Number of Days that Out-of-Town Visitor Groups who would have visited regardless of the game Stayed Longer because of it (Extended Stayers)

Days	Number of Groups	Percentage
0	129	95%
1	5	4%
2	2	1%

Table 4 Group Size

Number in the Immediate Group	Out-of-Towners		Extended Stayers	
	Number of Groups	Percentage	Number of Groups	Percentage
1	4	4%	1	17%
2	43	41%	1	17%
3	15	15%	1	17%
4 or more	42	40%	3	50%
Mean Size	5.09		3.67	

Table 5   Average Per Group Per Day Expenditures ($)

Items	Out-of-Towners		Extended Stayers	
	City C Area	Outside the City C Area	City C Area	Outside the City C Area
Food and Beverages	19.79	3.21	5.85	4.70
Night Clubs, Lounges & Bars	3.18	0.00	3.93	3.16
Retail Shopping	3.69	0.41	6.33	1.25
Lodging Expenses	0.00	0.00	21.57	2.49
Private Auto Expenses	2.34	1.30	0.00	1.25
Commercial Transportation	0.00	0.00	0.00	2.49
Other Expenses	0.00	0.00	0.00	0.00
Total	29.00	4.92	37.67	15.34

Table 6   Total Direct Expenditures ($)

Items	Out-of-Towners		Extended Stayers	
	City C Area	Outside the City C Area	City C Area	Outside the City C Area
Food and Beverages	17,215	2,791	470	378
Night Clubs, Lounges, Bars	2,763	0	316	254
Retail Shopping	3,205	359	509	100
Lodging Expenses	0	0	1,734	200
Private Auto Expenses	2,039	1,133	0	100
Commercial Transportation	0	0	0	200
Other Expenses	0	0	0	0
Total	25,222	4,283	3,029	1,233

Table 7   Economic Impact of Out-of-Town Visitors on Sales

Items	Sales Coefficient				Impact on Sales ($)
	Direct	Indirect	Induced	Total	
Food & Beverages	1	0.2638	0.6652	1.9290	33,207
Night Clubs, Lounges & Bars	1	0.2638	0.6652	1.9290	5,330
Retail Shopping	1	0.2061	0.8501	2.0562	6,591
Lodging Expenses	1	0.3618	0.5766	1.9384	0
Private Auto Expenses	1	0.2161	0.3199	1.5360	3,132
Commercial Transportation	1	0.2821	0.3349	1.6169	0
Other Expenses	1	0.3208	0.8161	2.1370	0
Total					48,260

Table 8   Economic Impact of Extended Stayers on Sales

Items	Sales Coefficient				Impact on Sales ($)
	Direct	Indirect	Induced	Total	
Food & Beverages	1	0.2638	0.6652	1.9290	907
Night Clubs, Lounges & Bars	1	0.2638	0.6652	1.9290	610
Retail Shopping	1	0.2061	0.8501	2.0562	1,046
Lodging Expenses	1	0.3618	0.5766	1.9384	3,362
Private Auto Expenses	1	0.2161	0.3199	1.5360	0
Commercial Transportation	1	0.2821	0.3349	1.6169	0
Other Expenses	1	0.3208	0.8161	2.1370	0
Total					5,924

Table 9   Economic Impact of Out-of-Town Visitors on Personal Income

Items	Personal Income Coefficient				Impact on Personal Income ($)
	Direct	Indirect	Induced	Total	
Food & Beverages	0.3293	0.0727	0.2238	0.6258	10,773
Night Clubs, Lounges & Bars	0.3293	0.0727	0.2238	0.6258	1,729
Retail Shopping	0.3969	0.0585	0.2860	0.7413	2,376
Lodging Expenses	0.2946	0.1133	0.1940	0.6019	0
Private Auto Expenses	0.3340	0.0621	0.1076	0.5038	1,027
Commercial Transportation	0.2206	0.0910	0.1127	0.4243	0
Other Expenses	0.3164	0.0950	0.2746	0.6859	0
Total					15,905

Table 10   Economic Impact of Extended Stayers on Personal Income

Items	Personal Income Coefficient				Impact on Personal Income ($)
	Direct	Indirect	Induced	Total	
Food & Beverages	0.3293	0.0727	0.2238	0.6258	294
Night Clubs, Lounges & Bars	0.3293	0.0727	0.2238	0.6258	198
Retail Shopping	0.3969	0.0585	0.2860	0.7413	377
Lodging Expenses	0.2946	0.1133	0.1940	0.6019	1,044
Private Auto Expenses	0.3340	0.0621	0.1076	0.5038	0
Commercial Transportation	0.2206	0.0910	0.1127	0.4243	0
Other Expenses	0.3164	0.0950	0.2746	0.6859	0
Total					1,913

Table 11 Economic Impact of Out-of-Town Visitors on Employment

Items	Employment Coefficient				Impact on Employment (people) *
	Direct	Indirect	Induced	Total	
Food & Beverages	32.0603	3.2179	10.3895	45.6677	0.79
Night Clubs, Lounges & Bars	32.0603	3.2179	10.3895	45.6677	0.13
Retail Shopping	42.4599	2.6203	13.2762	58.3564	0.19
Lodging Expenses	25.1385	5.4411	9.0058	39.5853	0.00
Private Auto Expenses	14.1410	2.8217	4.9956	21.9583	0.04
Commercial Transportation	13.3297	4.4286	5.2299	22.9882	0.00
Other Expenses	38.7726	4.5068	12.7459	56.0252	0.00
Total					1.14

Table 12 Economic Impact of Extended Stayers on Employment

Items	Employment Coefficient				Impact on Employment (people) *
	Direct	Indirect	Induced	Total	
Food & Beverages	32.0603	3.2179	10.3895	45.6677	0.02
Night Clubs, Lounges & Bars	32.0603	3.2179	10.3895	45.6677	0.01
Retail Shopping	42.4599	2.6203	13.2762	58.3564	0.03
Lodging Expenses	25.1385	5.4411	9.0058	39.5853	0.07
Private Auto Expenses	14.1410	2.8217	4.9956	21.9583	0.00
Commercial Transportation	13.3297	4.4286	5.2299	22.9882	0.00
Other Expenses	38.7726	4.5068	12.7459	56.0252	0.00
Total					0.13

* This figure refers to both full-time and part-time jobs. It assumes the local economy is operating at full capacity and that there is no slack to absorb additional demand created by these events

1. Driver, B.L. and D.H. Bruns. 1999. Concepts and uses of the benefits approach to leisure. In *Leisure studies at the millennium*, edited by T. Burton and E. Jackson. State College, PA: Venture Publishing.

2. Godbey, G. 1991. Redefining public parks and recreation. *Parks and Recreation* 26(10): 58-61,74.

3. Crompton, J.L. 1999. *Financing and acquiring park and recreation resources*. Champaign, IL: Human Kinetics

4. Ries, A. and J. Trout. 1981. *Positioning: The battle for your mind*. New York: McGraw-Hill.

5. Glyptis, S. 1989. *Leisure and unemployment*. Milton Keynes, England: Open University.

6. Godbey, G. 1994. Extraordinary change: A few implications for recreation and parks. *TRAPS* Magazine, Spring: 16-18.

7. Kotler, P., D.H. Haider and I. Rein. 1993. *Marketing places: Attracting investment, industry, and tourism to cities, states and nations*. New York: Free Press.

8. Godbey, G. 1993. The contribution of recreation and parks to reducing health care costs: From theory to practice. *Trends* 30(4): 37-41.

9. Smith, S.L.J. and D. Wilton. 1997. TSAs and the WTTC/WEFA methodology: different satellites or different planets? *Tourism Economics* 3(3): 279-263.

10. Curtis, G. 1993 September. Waterlogged. *Texas Monthly*, 7.

11. Archer, B.H. 1984. Economic impact: Misleading multiplier. *Annals of Tourism Research* 11(3): 517-518.

12. Ap, J. and J.L. Crompton. 1998. Development and testing of a tourism impact scale. *Journal of Travel Research* 37(2): 120-130.

13. Economics Research Associates. 1986. *Community Economic Impact of the 1984 Olympic Games in Los Angeles*. Los Angeles: Economic Research Associates.

14. Burns, J.P.A. and T.J. Mules. 1986. An economic evaluation of the Adelaide Grand Prix. In G.J. Syme, B.J. Shaw, P.M. Fenton and W.S. Mueller (Eds.). *The planning and evaluation of hallmark events*: 172-185. Aldershot, England: Avebury.

15. Irwin, R.L., P. Wang and W.A. Sutton. 1996. Comparative analysis of diaries and projected spending to assess patron expenditure behavior at short-term sporting events. *Festival Management and Event Tourism* 4(1/2): 29-38.

16. Minnesota IMPLAN Group. 1997. *IMPLAN professional: Social accounting & impact analysis software.* Stillwater, Minnesota: MIG Inc.

17. Delpy, L. and M. Li. 1998. The art and science of conducting economic impact studies. *Journal of Vacation Marketing* 4(3): 230-254.